DAY OF THE DEAD
DOT-TO-DOT

DAY OF THE DEAD
DOT-TO-DOT

MADDY BROOK

ARCTURUS

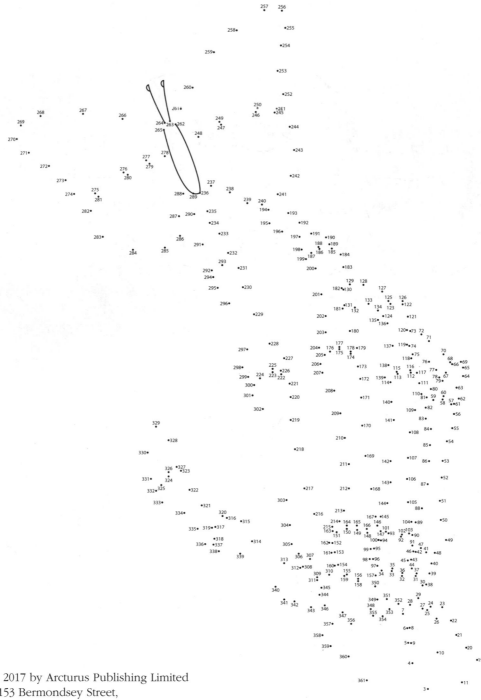

This edition published in 2017 by Arcturus Publishing Limited
26/27 Bickels Yard, 151–153 Bermondsey Street,
London SE1 3HA

Copyright © Arcturus Holdings Limited

ISBN: 978-1-78428-604-0
CH005429NT
Supplier 29, Date 0317, Print Run 5915

Printed in China
Created for children 10+

INTRODUCTION

The 'Day of the Dead', or *Día de los Muertos* as it is known in Spanish, is a Mexican holiday that dates back thousands of years and was even thought to be celebrated by the Ancient Aztecs, Incas, Mayans, and other tribes. The holiday marks the day when the spirits of the departed make their annual trip back to Earth. Today, it is characterized by vibrant imagery featuring skeletons, flowers, and intricate patterns. People will often decorate their houses with sugar skulls, detailed paper cut-outs, and shrines to honor the souls of their lost loved ones. There is a great amount of dancing, with traditional Mexican Mariachi bands, beautiful dresses, and painted faces. People visit cemeteries and make altars in their homes covered with the departeds' favorite foods and objects for when they visit Earth.

These dot-to-dot puzzles bring a fresh perspective to these macabre artworks and are fun and easy to do. All you have to do is connect the dots. Each dot is numbered, so the first thing you have to do is find number one, then follow the sequence in ascending order. After that, what you do with the finished drawing is entirely up to you!

The illustrations in this book have 300–400 dots per image so they look intricate even before you start. There are more than 120 illustrations, from dancing skeletons to Mexican folk art. So open the book anywhere, grab a pen, or a nice, sharp pencil, and get started!

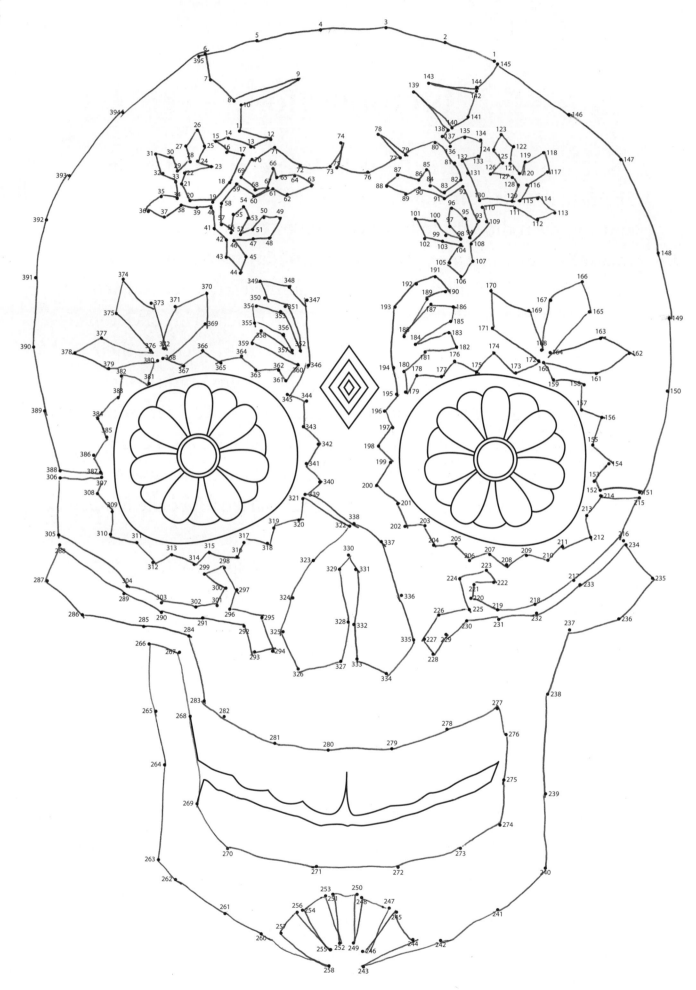

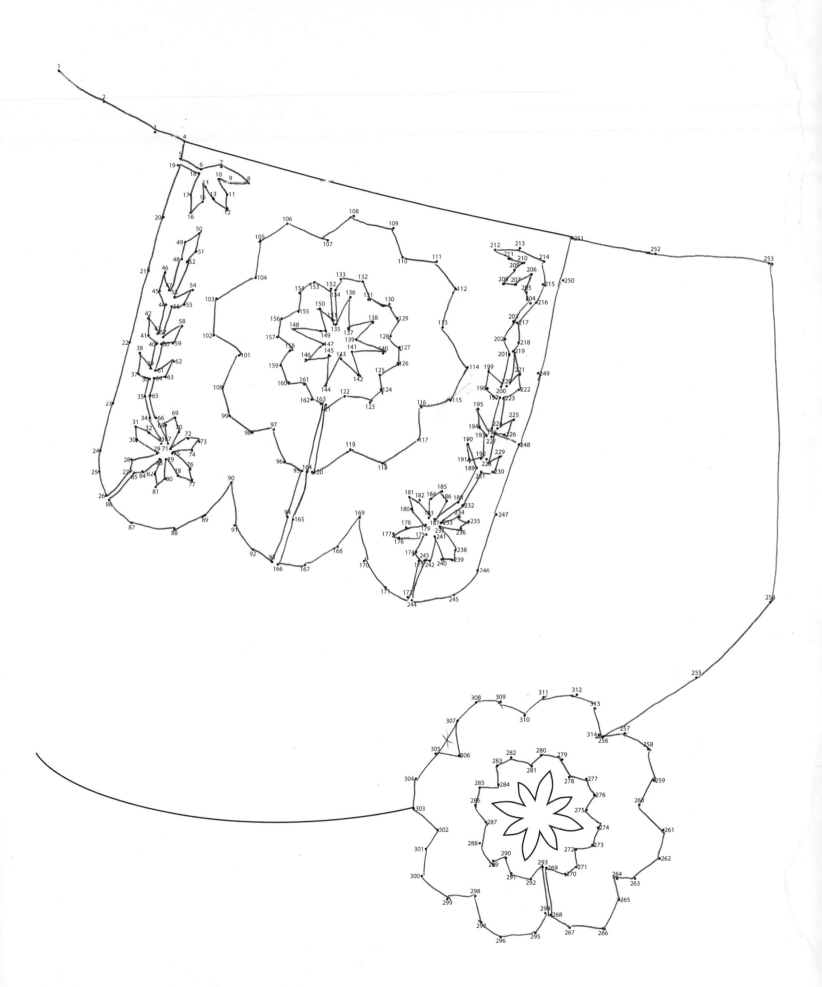

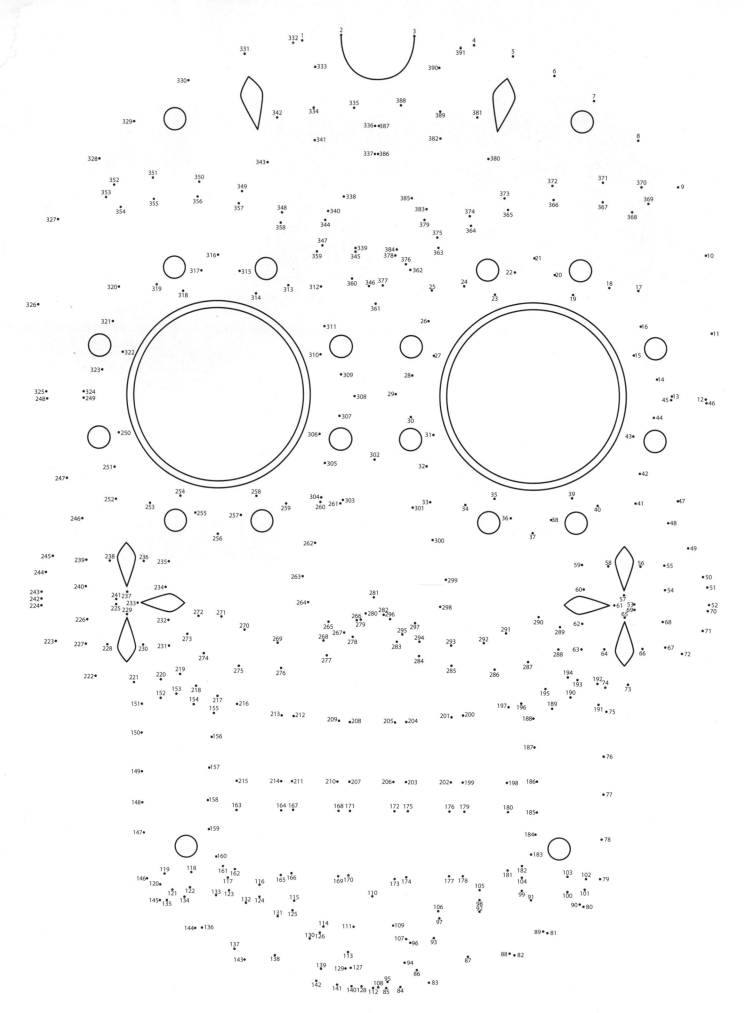

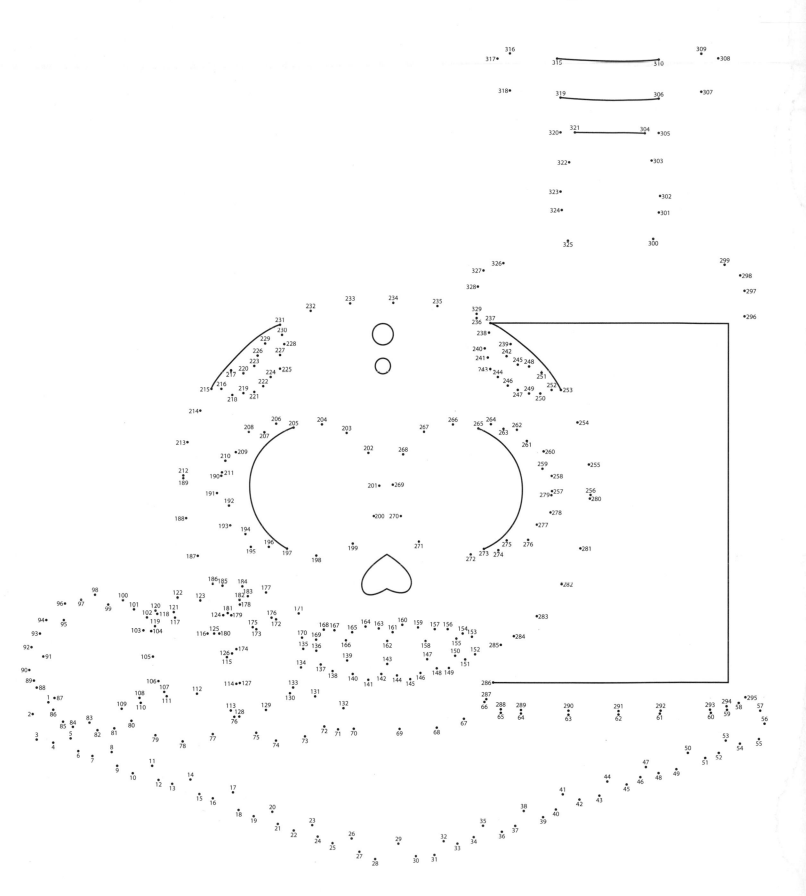

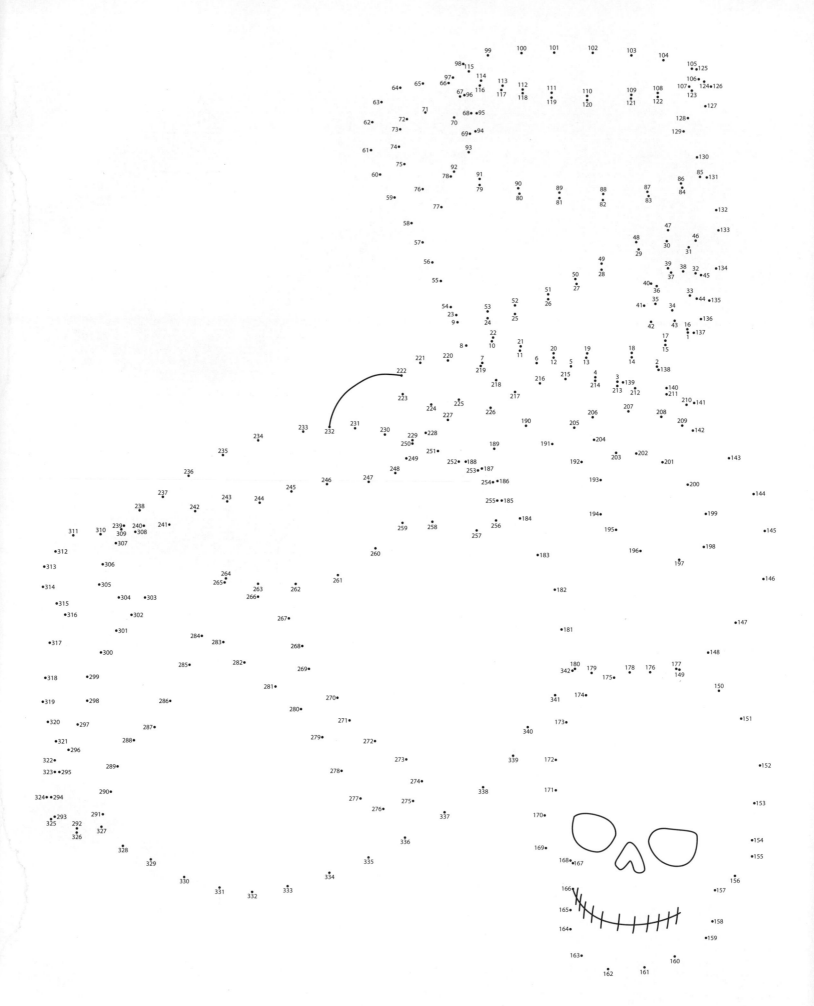

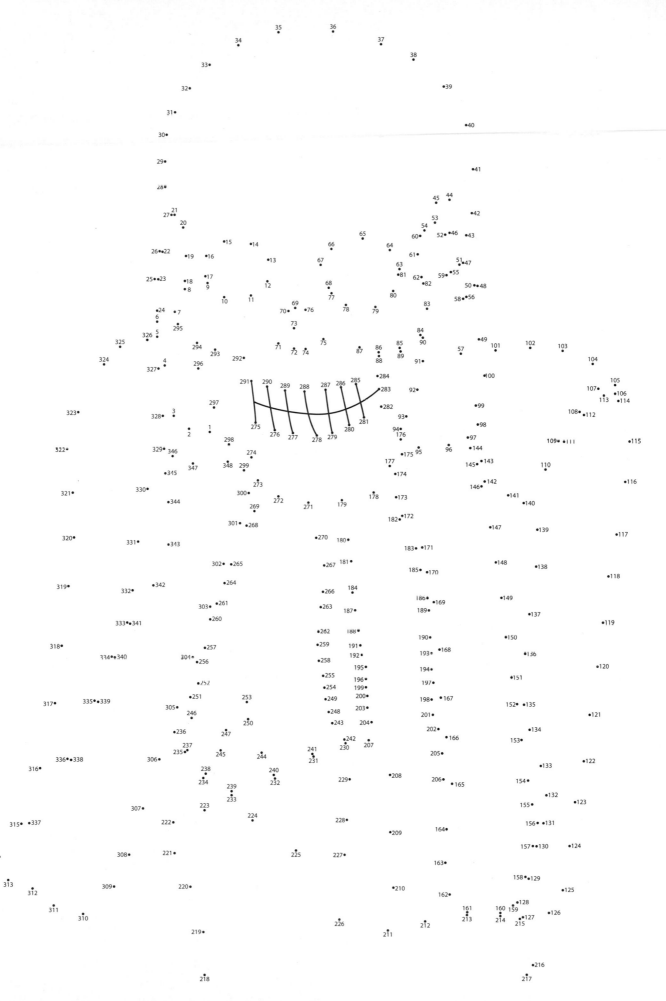

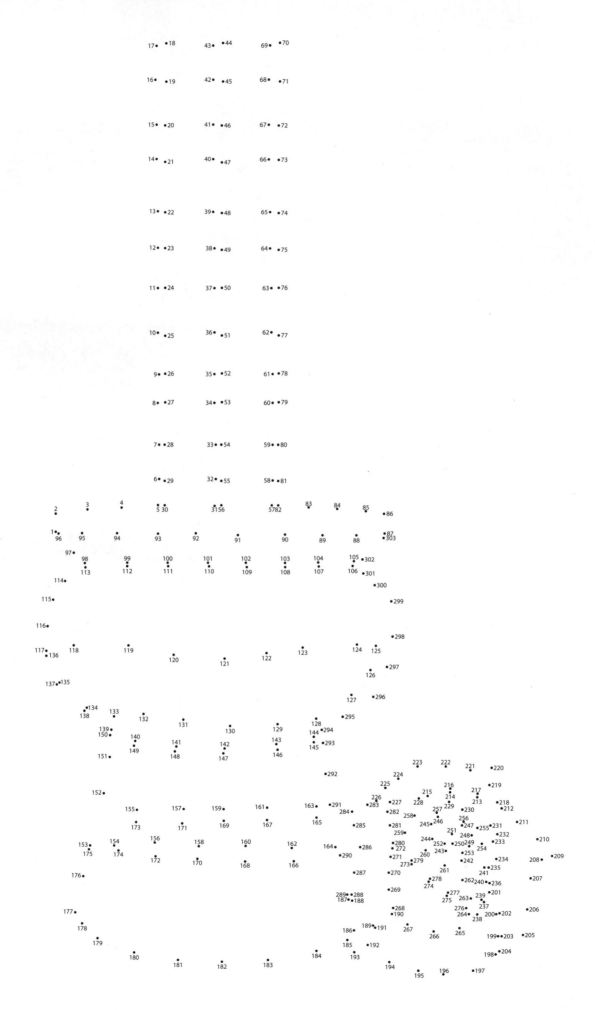

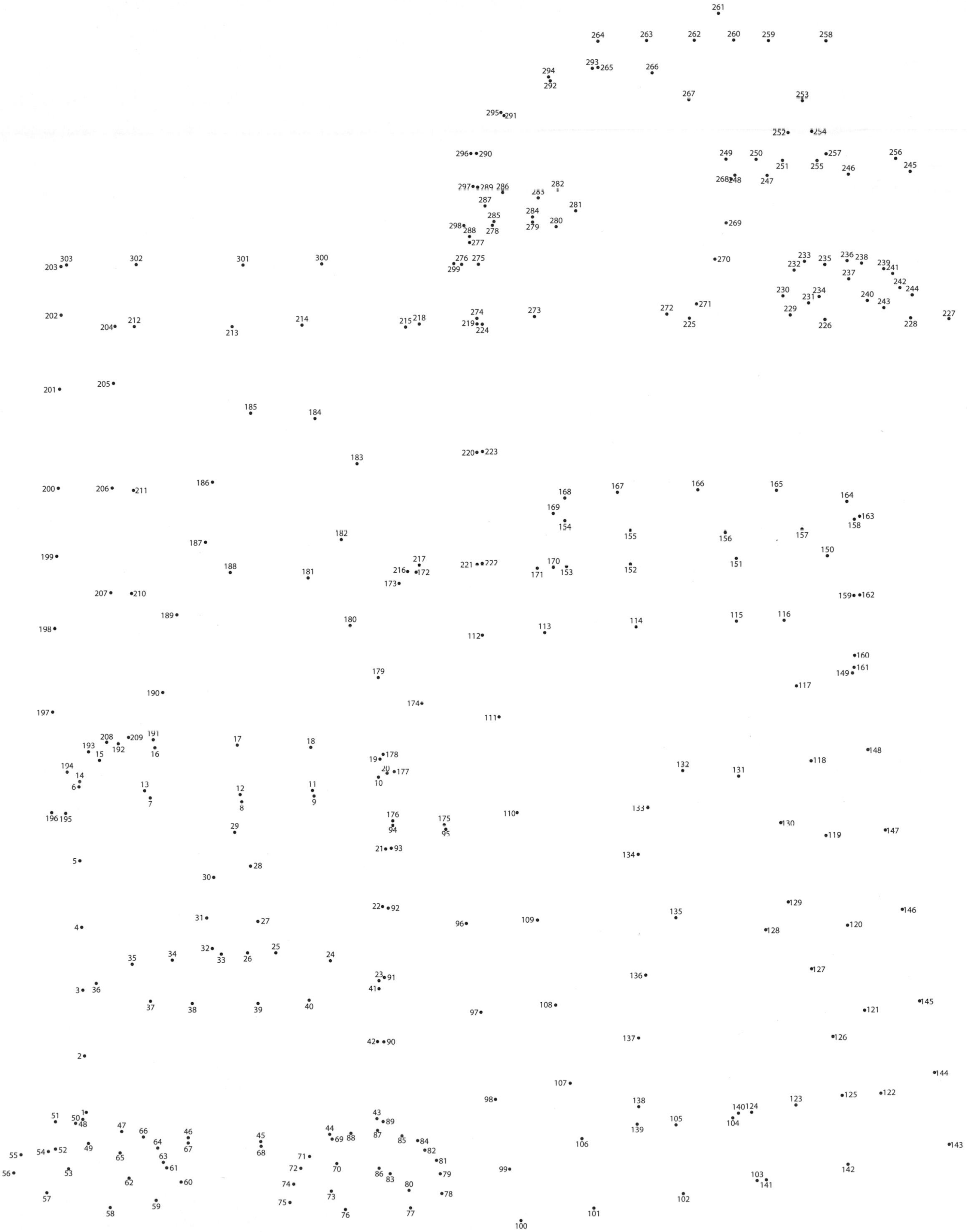

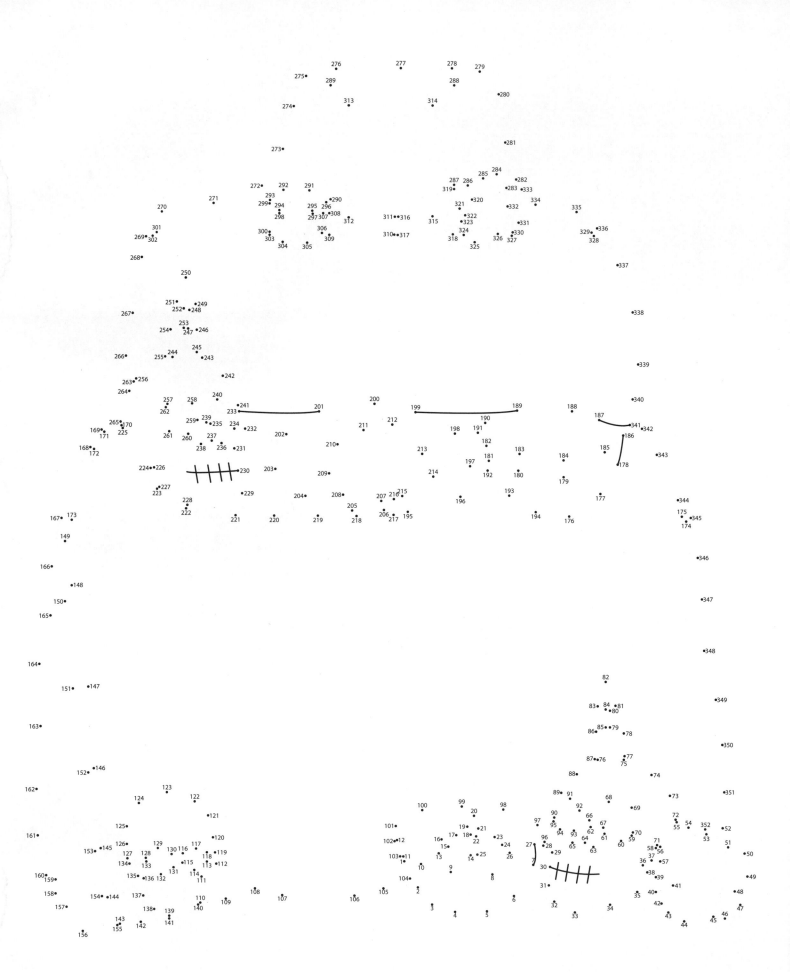

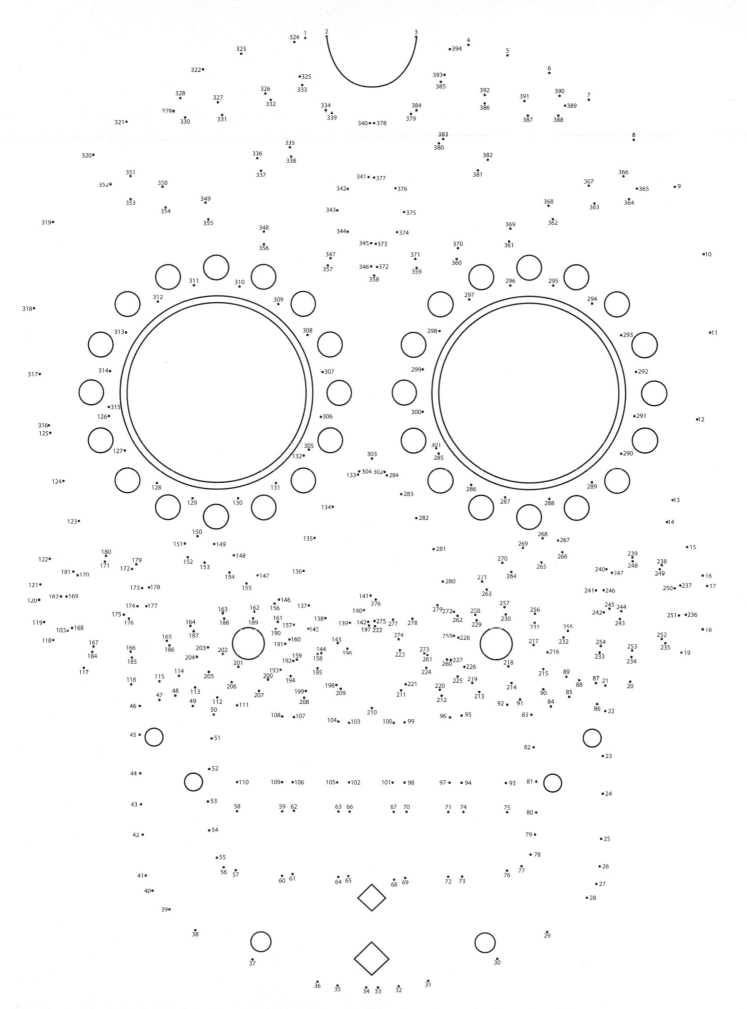

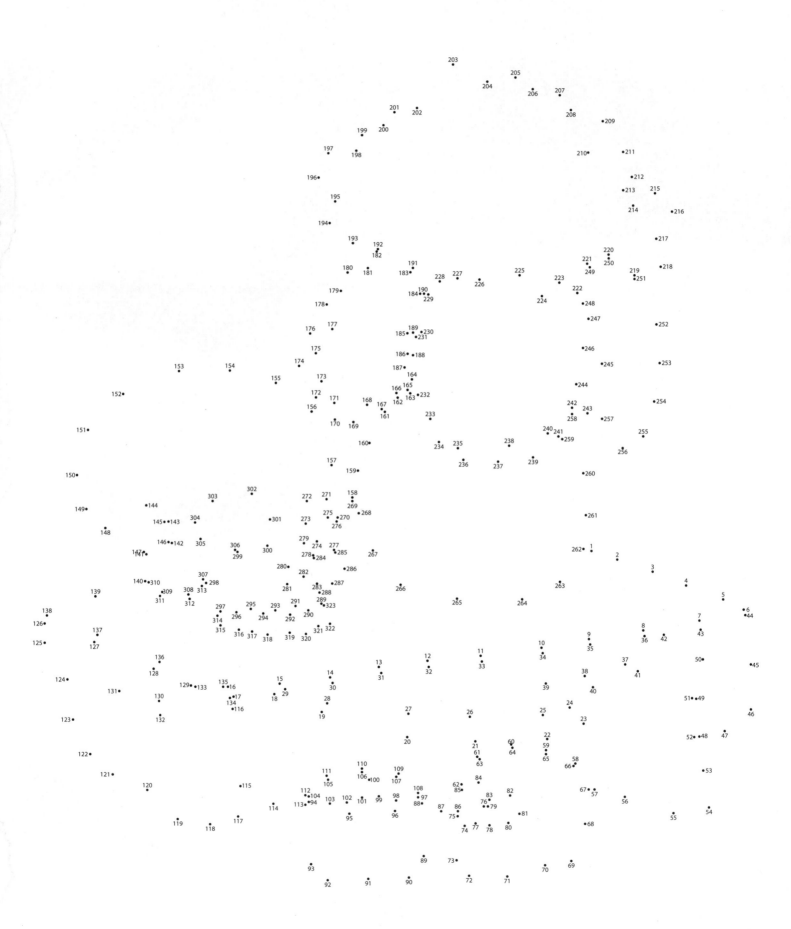

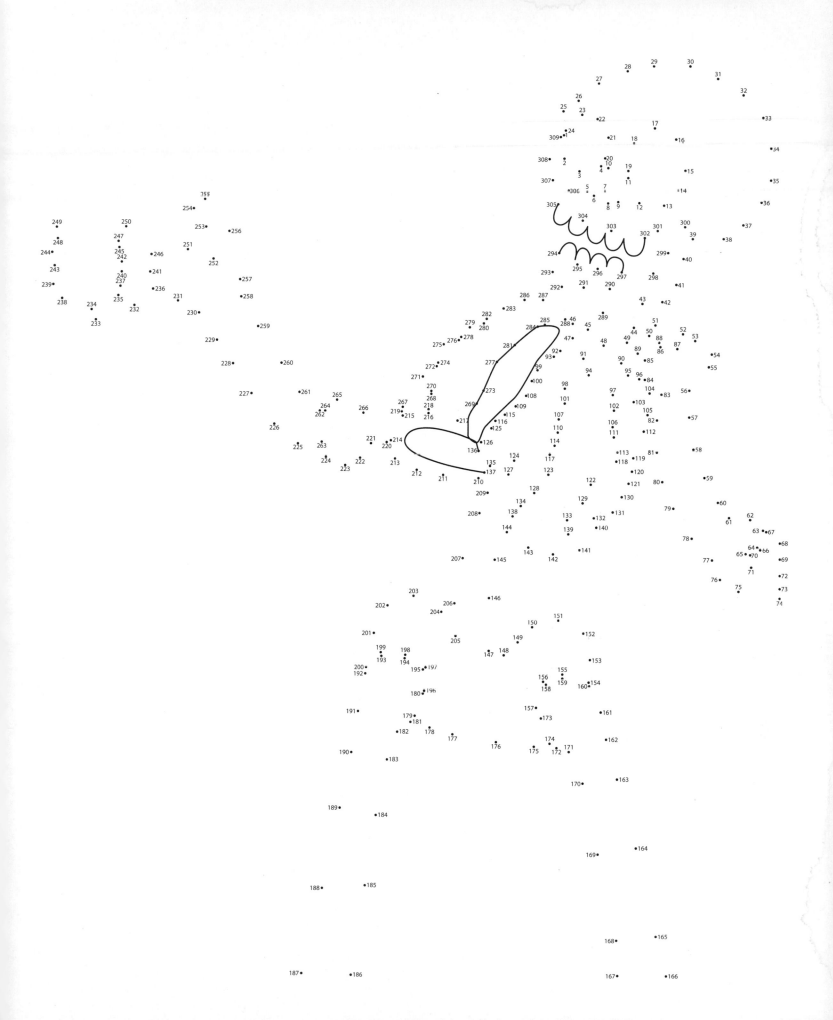

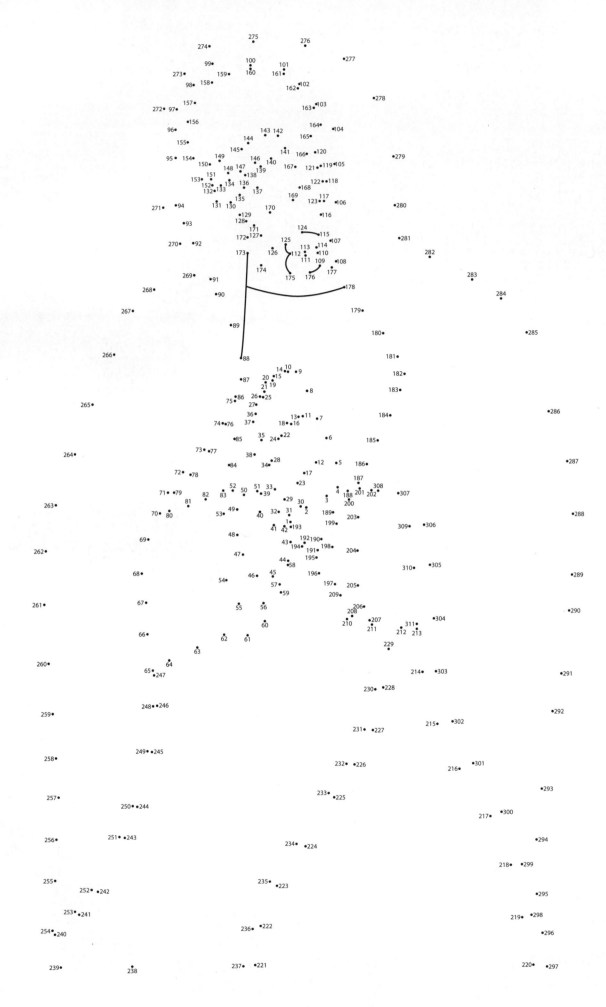

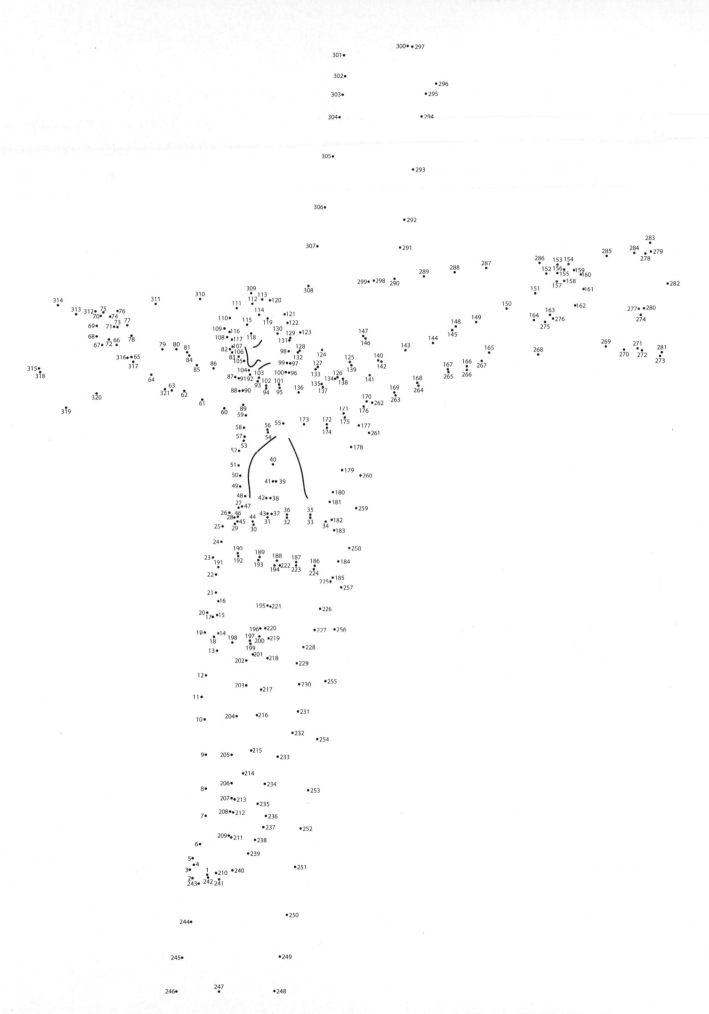

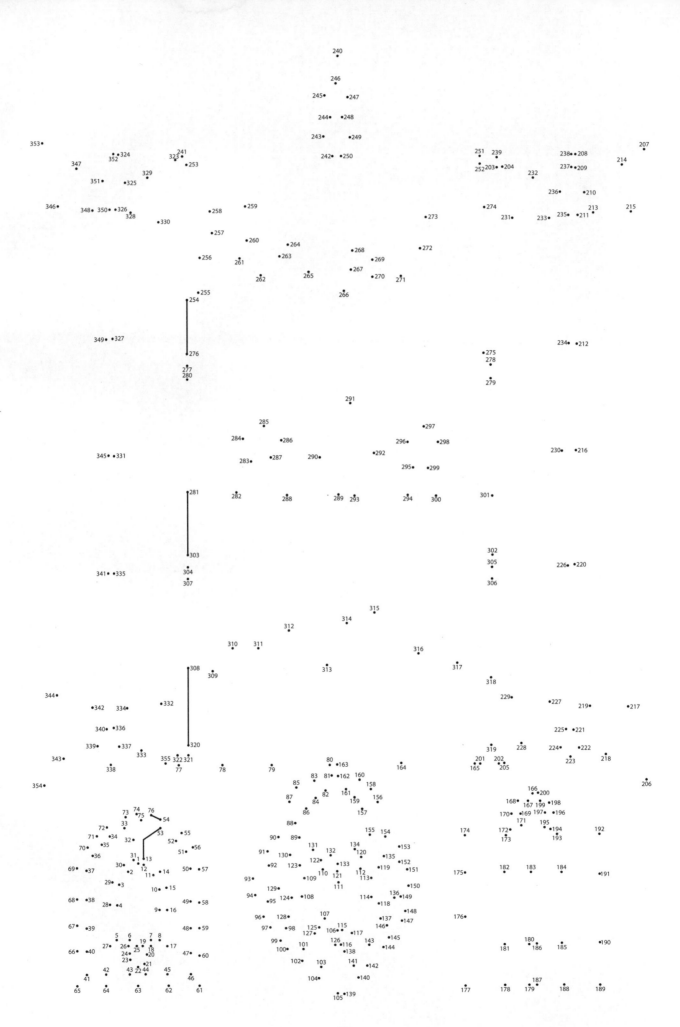

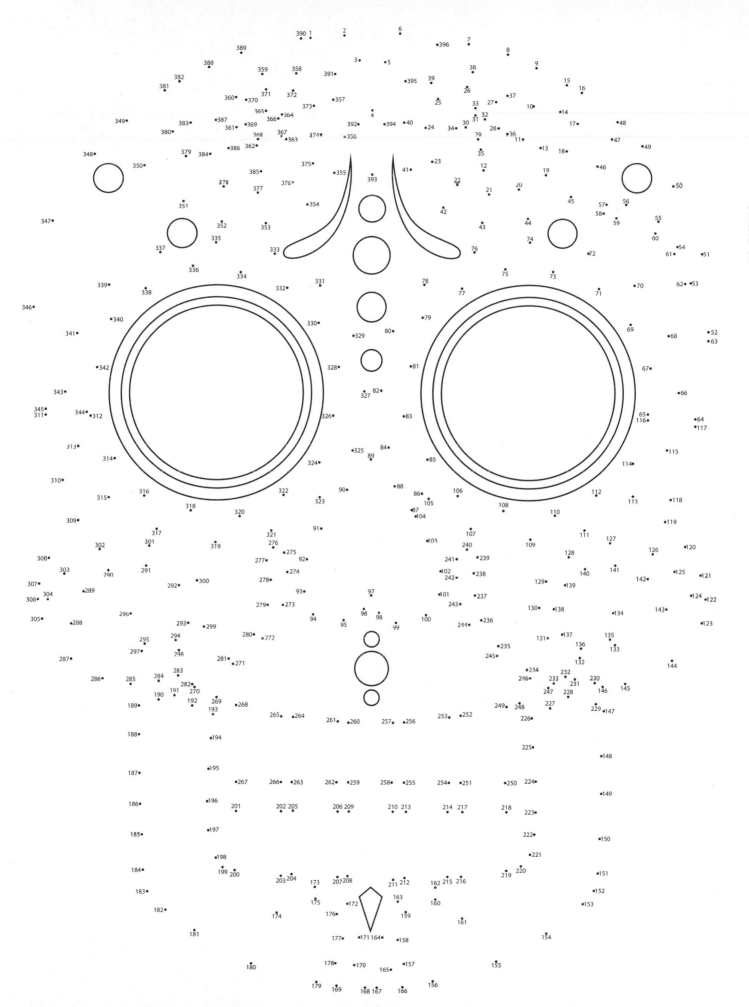

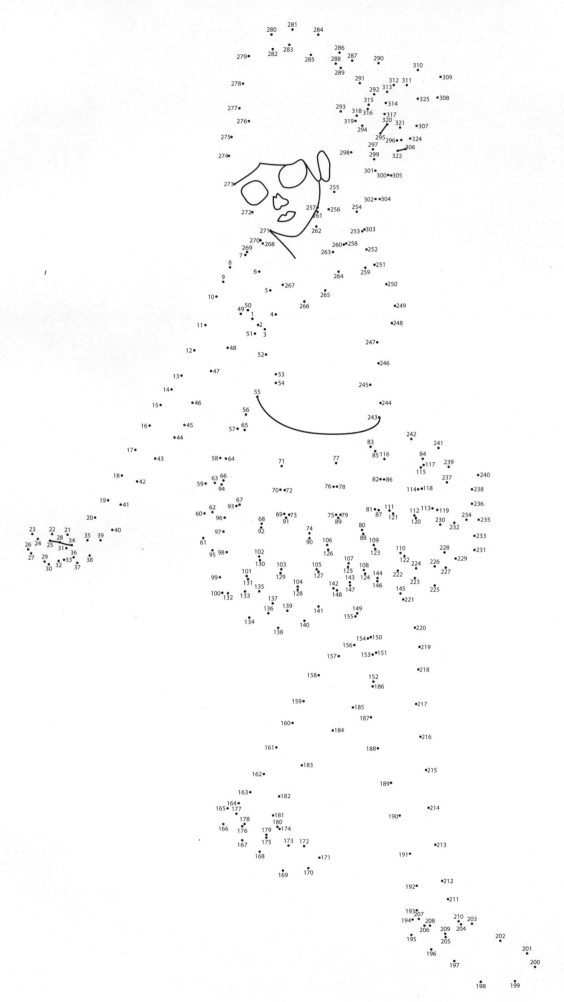

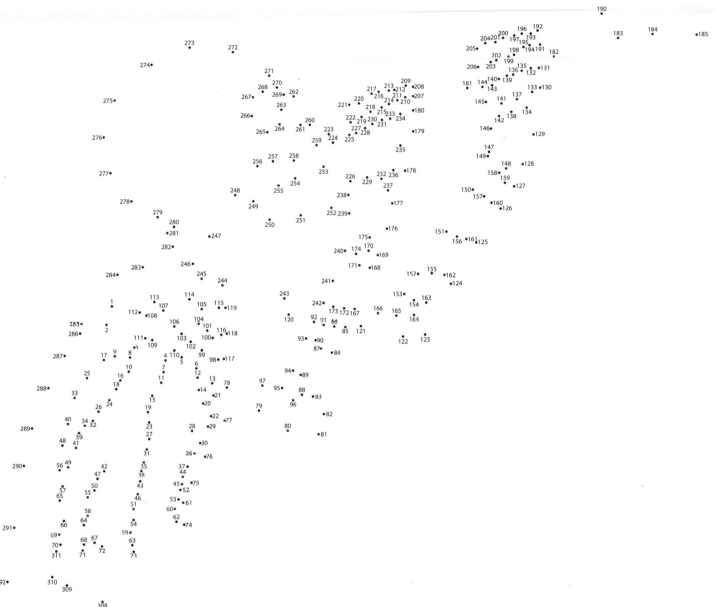

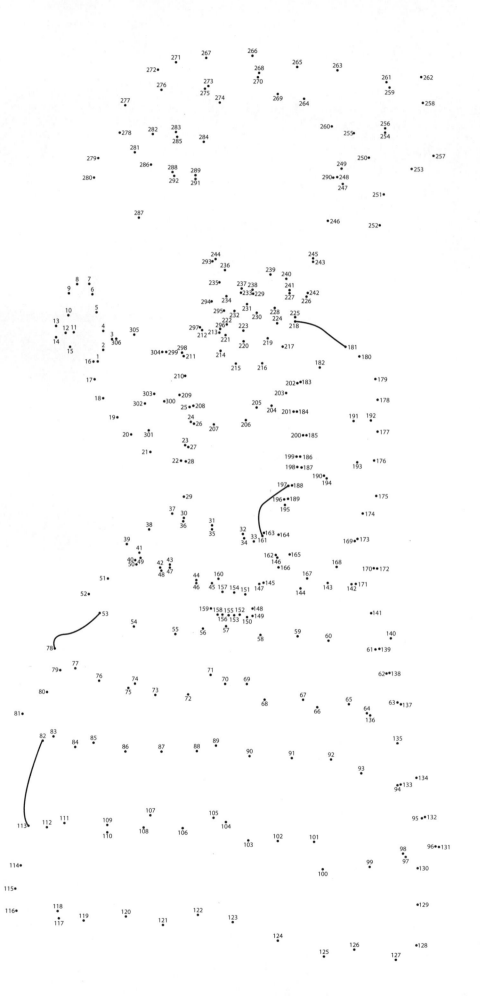

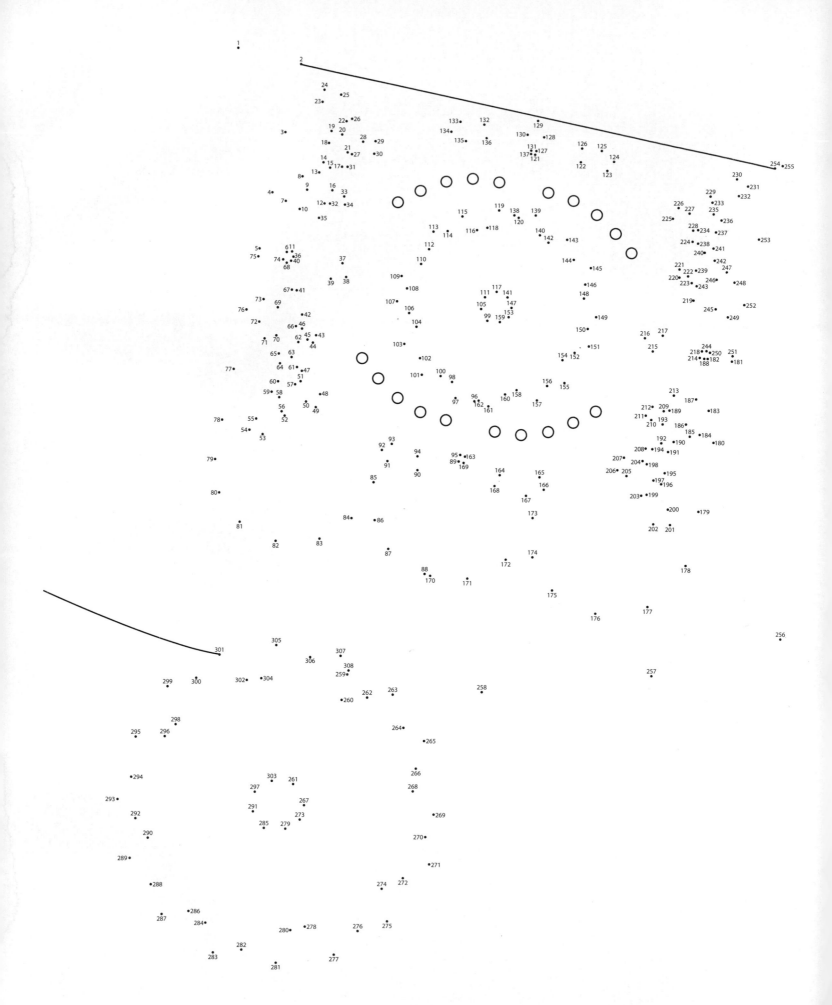

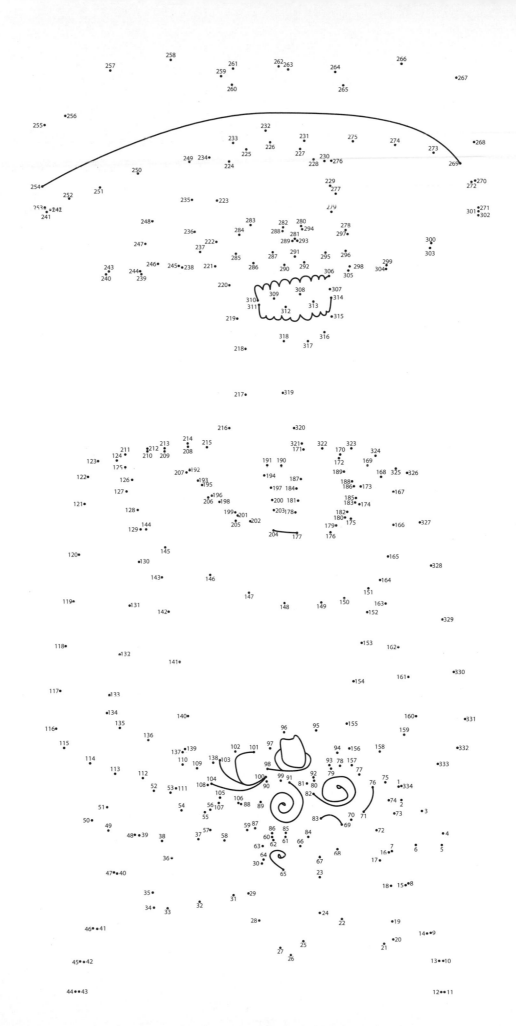

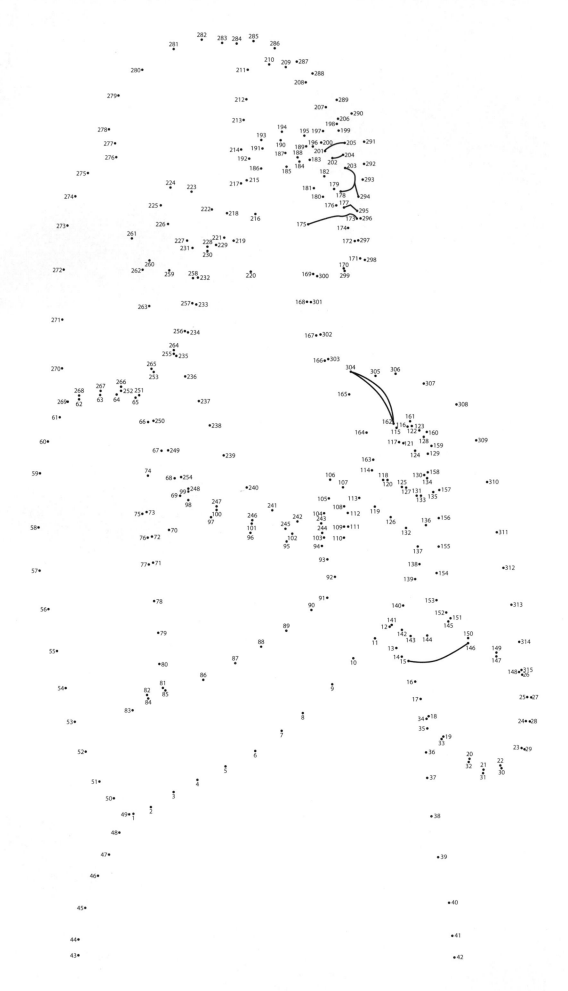

251•   •252

250•   •253

                        248
249•   •254
246•   247

              69   68   67   66
         157   169   •255
245•   •158 •168 •256
244•   70• 160• 159 167•166
            •156   170• •65
              161• •165
     •71 •155
243• 162•   •164 171• •64   •258
242•   •259
     72• •154
241•   •73 •153   172• •63   •257
236• 235 152• 163 173• •62 265
         •74   •152   264   •260
240•   234• •75 •151   174• •61 •266   263•
237•   233• •76 •150   267• •60   268 269 262 271 55 54 53 •272
239• 238• 230 •125 124 •123 175•   59   270 56   261 182
228• 229   77   •122   58 57   180 181 •52
84• 83 82 81 80 79 78 149 126•   176   179   183•
143 144 145 146 147 148 •121   177 178
85• •142   127•
227•   128• •120
86• •141   129•   •119
140 139 138 137 136 135 134 133 130• •118   189
87 88 89 90 91 92 93 94 131• 115 116 117 190   188 187 186 185
226• 225• 211 210 209 132• 95 114   46   48 49 •50
223 224 212   191• 45 288   287 •274
                              44•   289• 286• 275 277•
208• •96 •113
213•   192• 43• 290•   •285   •279   •278
222• 221• 214• •207   291•
215• 206 •97   193• •42
220•   •98 •112   292• •284   •280
              •111   194• •41
216• 99 •110   •201
219•   195• •40
                                  •282
218• 100• •109   196• •39 •283
217••205   293
101• •108   197• •38 •294
204• 102• •107   198• •37 •295
203• 103• •106   199• •36 •296
202• 104• •105 201 33 34 200 35
30• 31 32 19 18 17 •297
21• 20
29• 22• 5 6 7 8
                    •4   9• •16 •298
28• 23• •3   10• •15 •299
27• 24• •2   11• •14
26• 25 1   12 13 •300

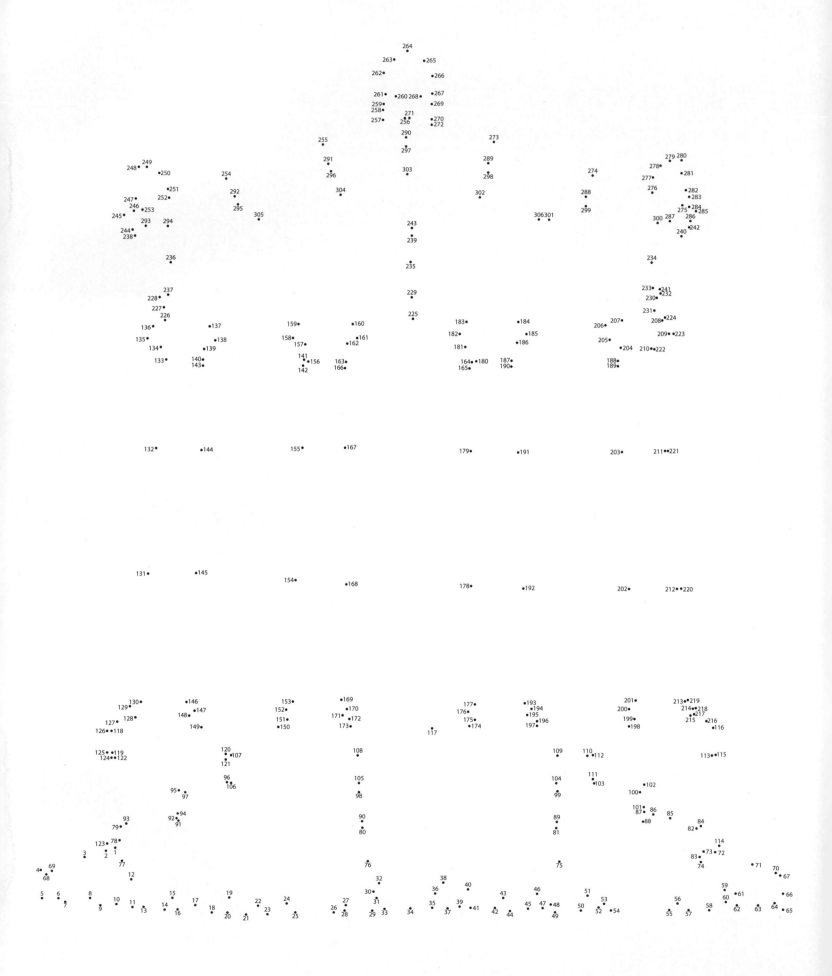

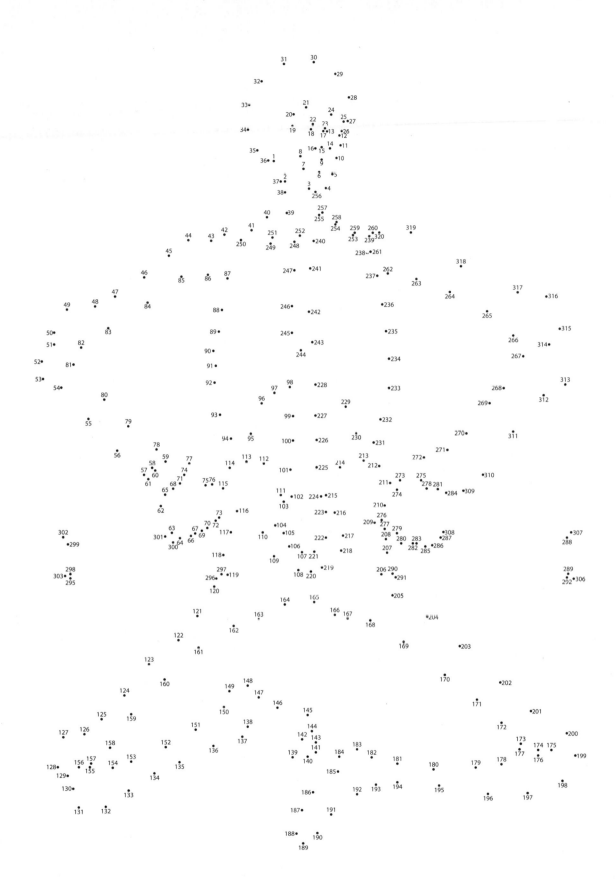

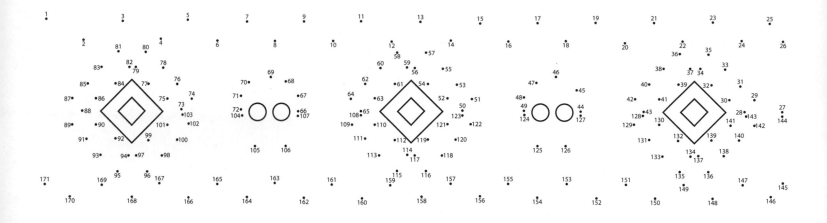

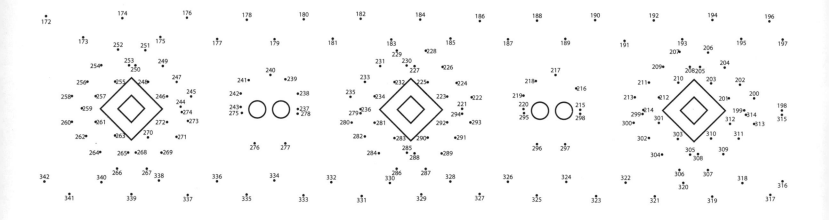

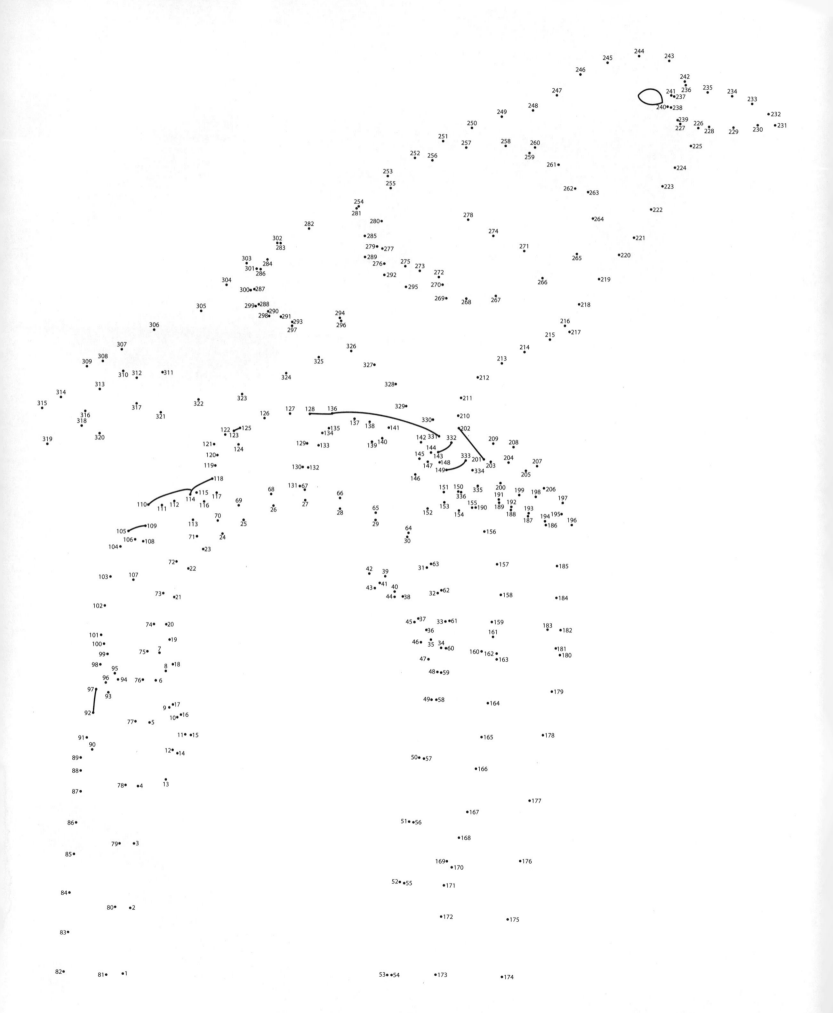

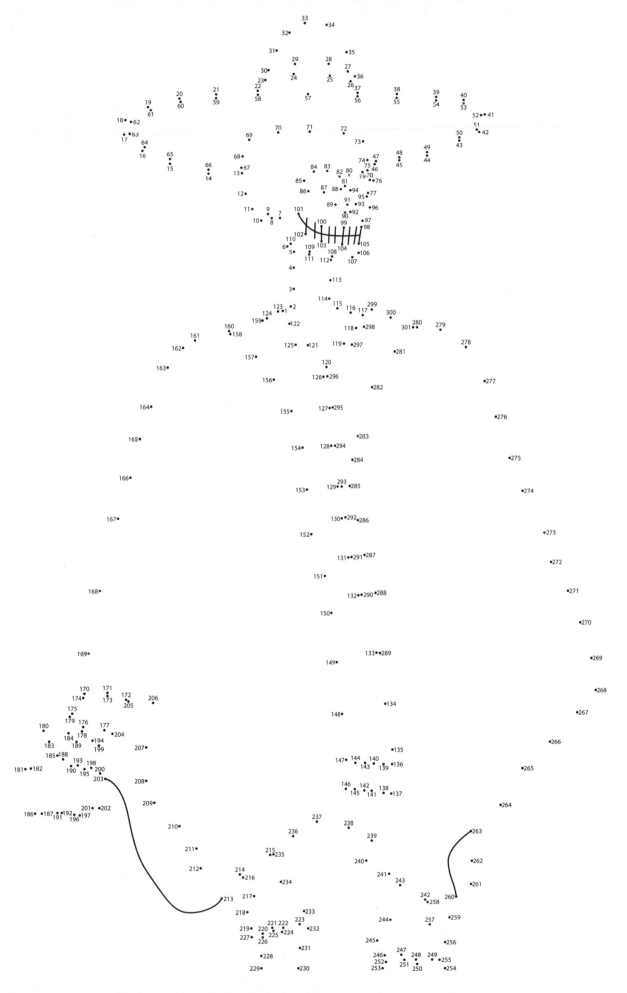

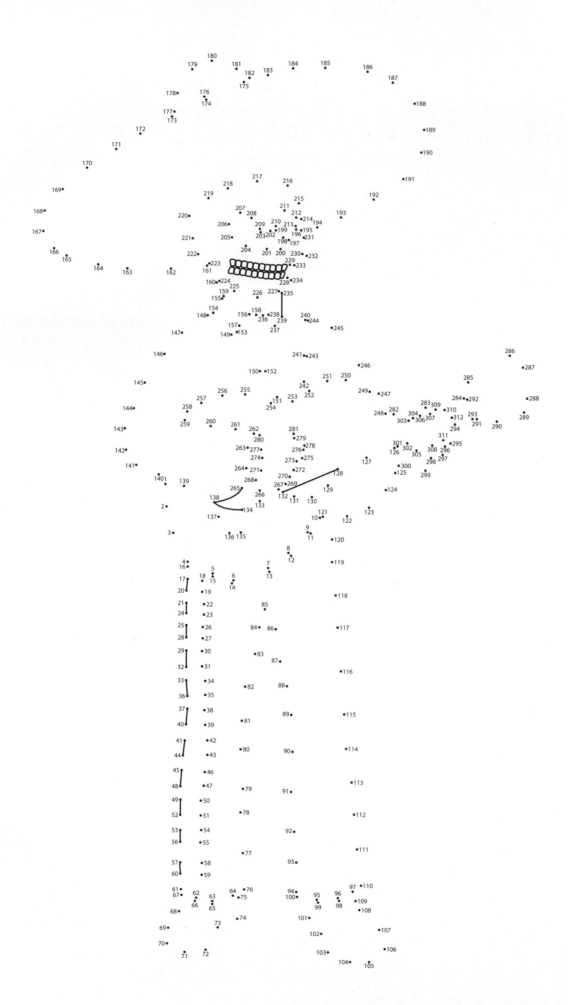

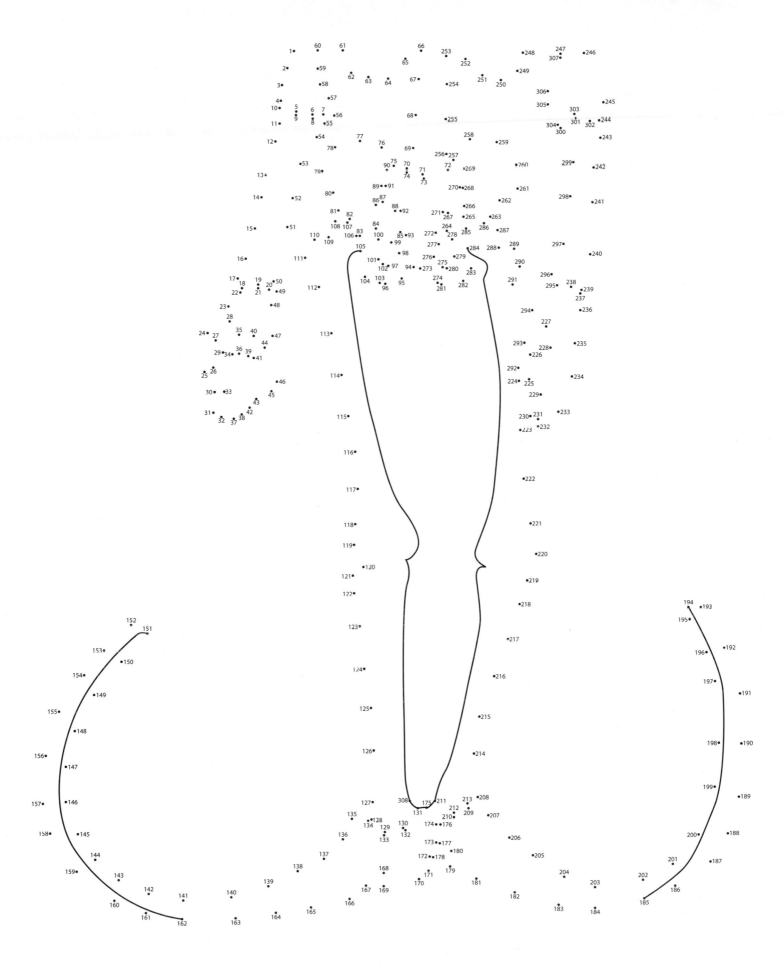

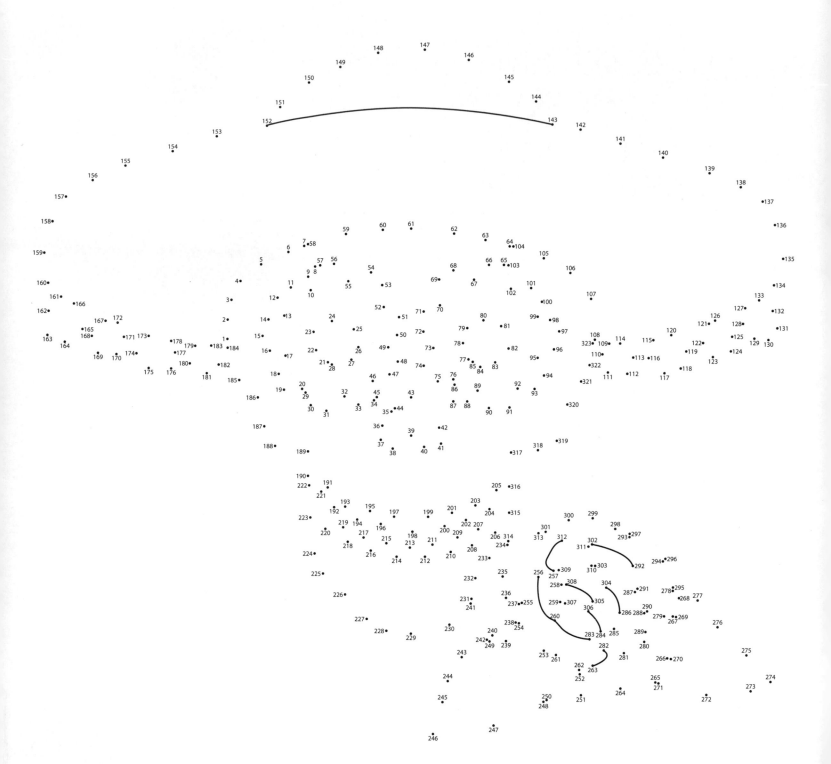

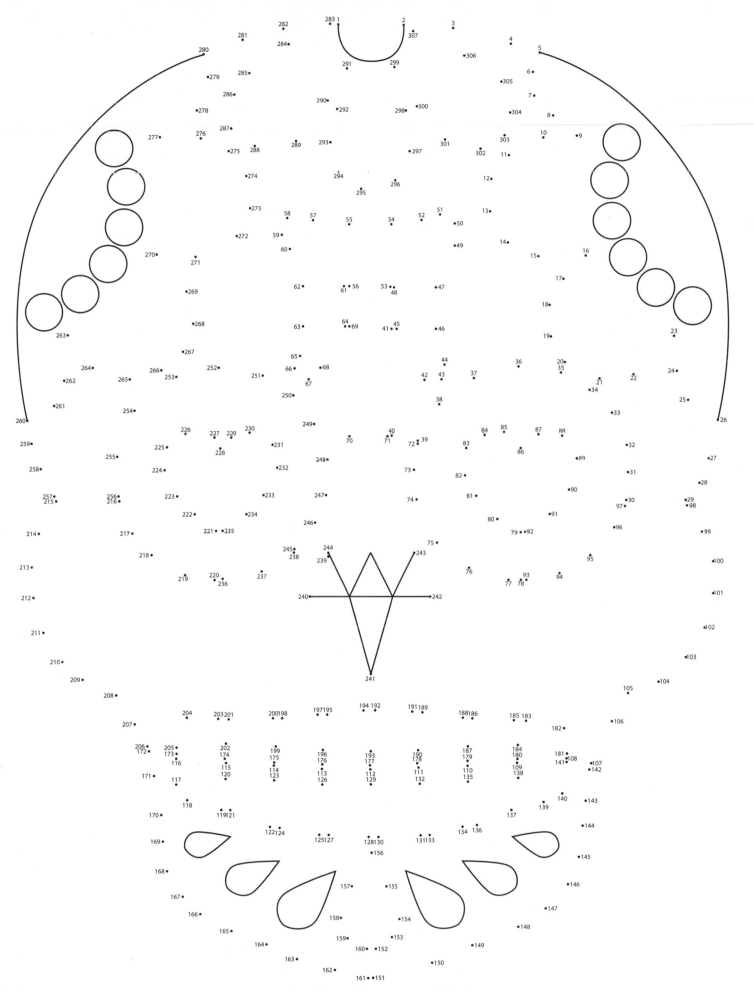

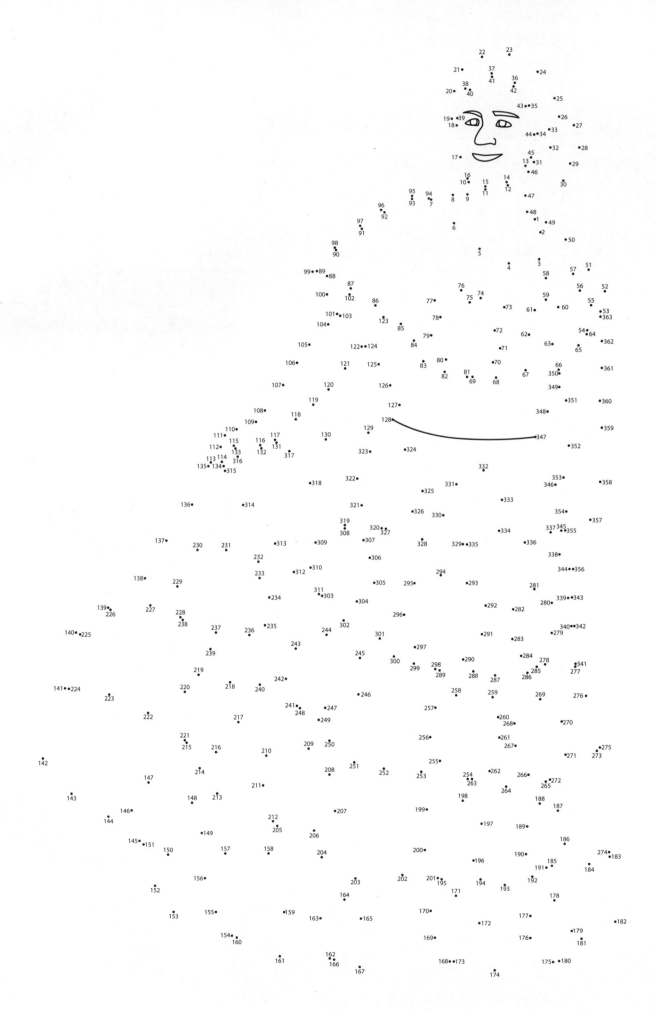

47

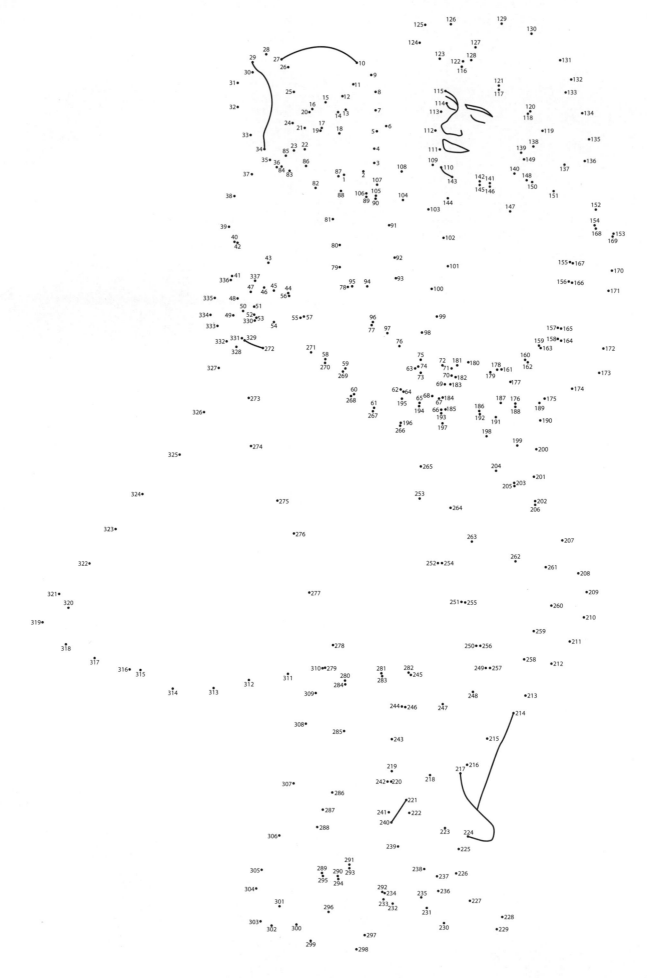

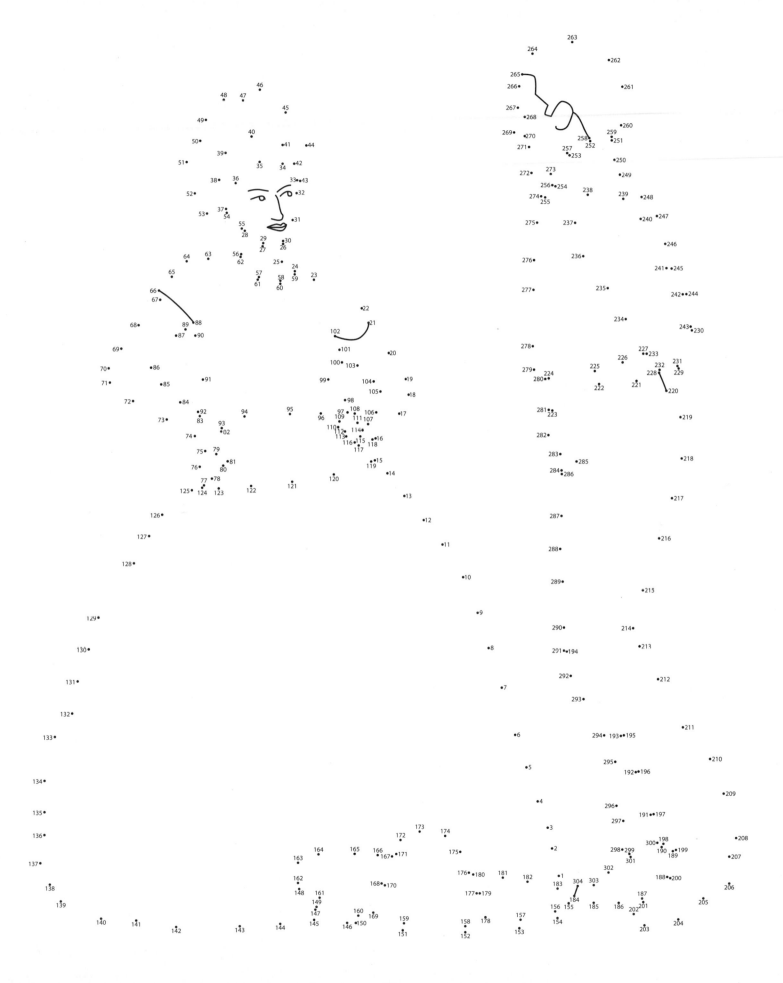

49

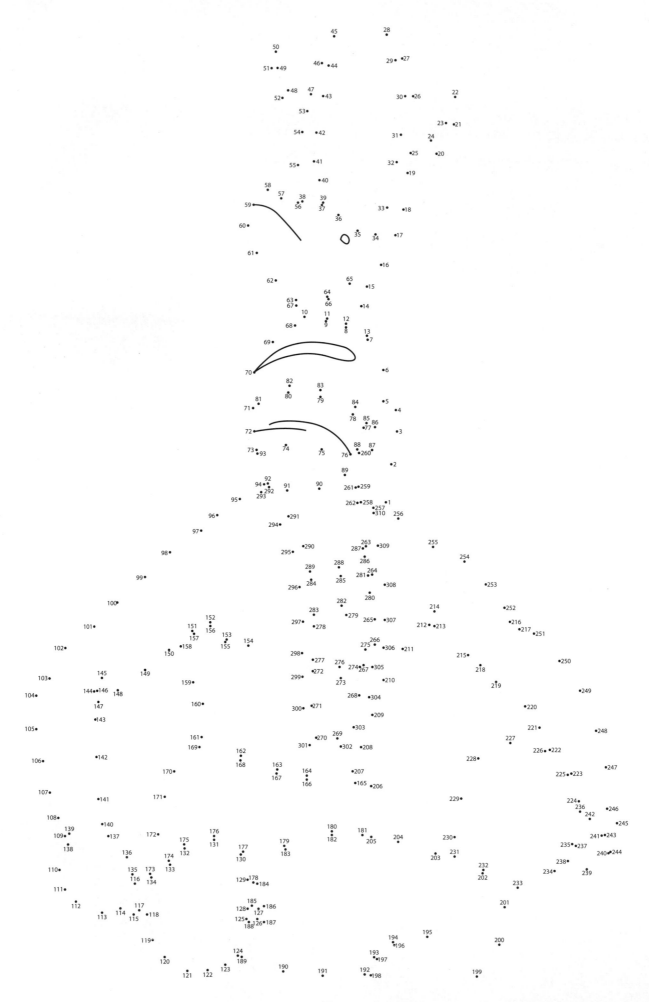

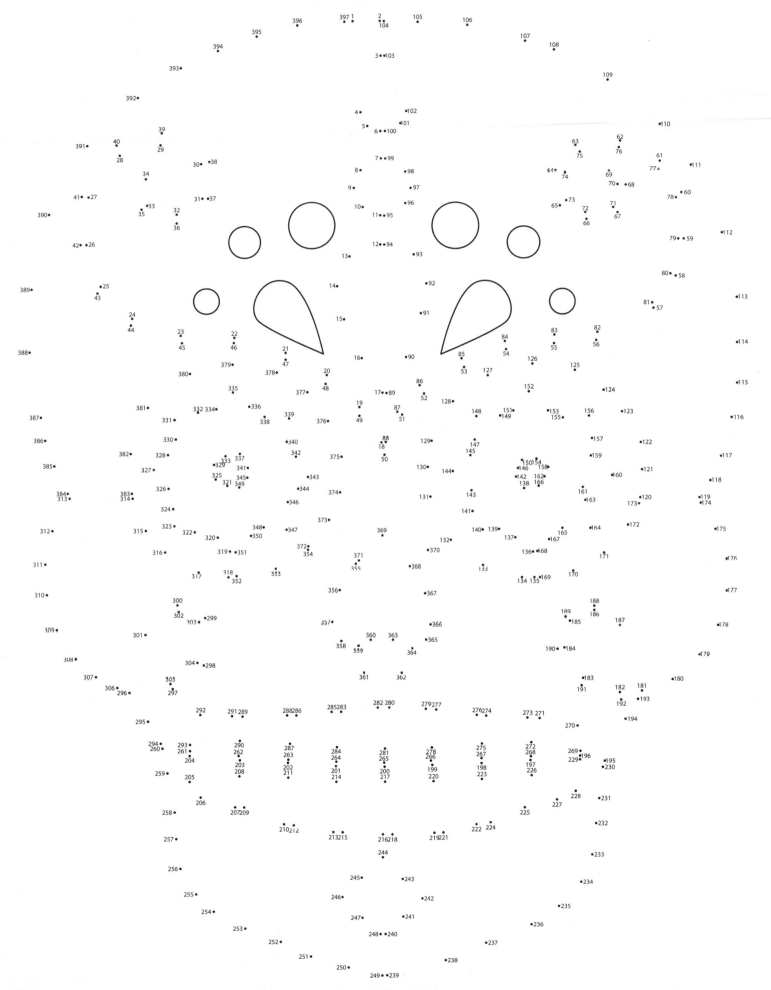

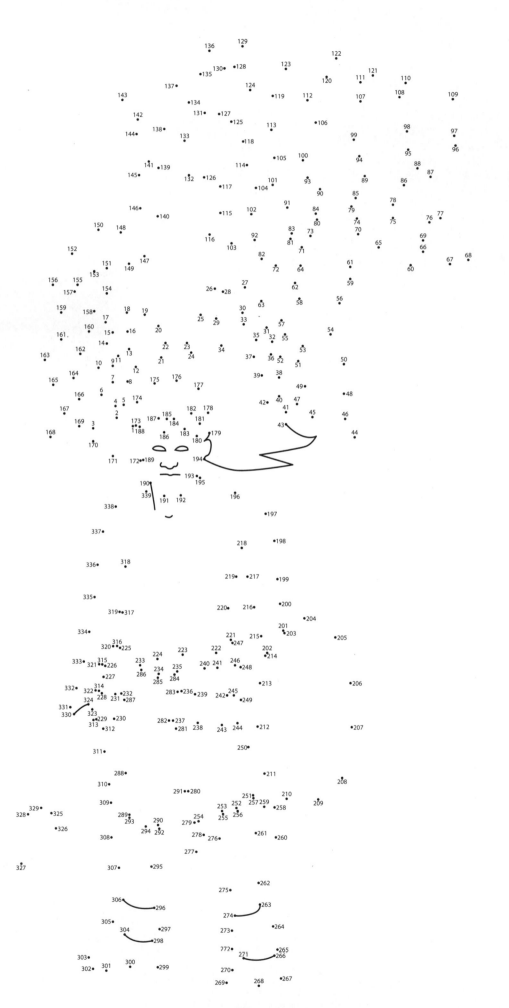

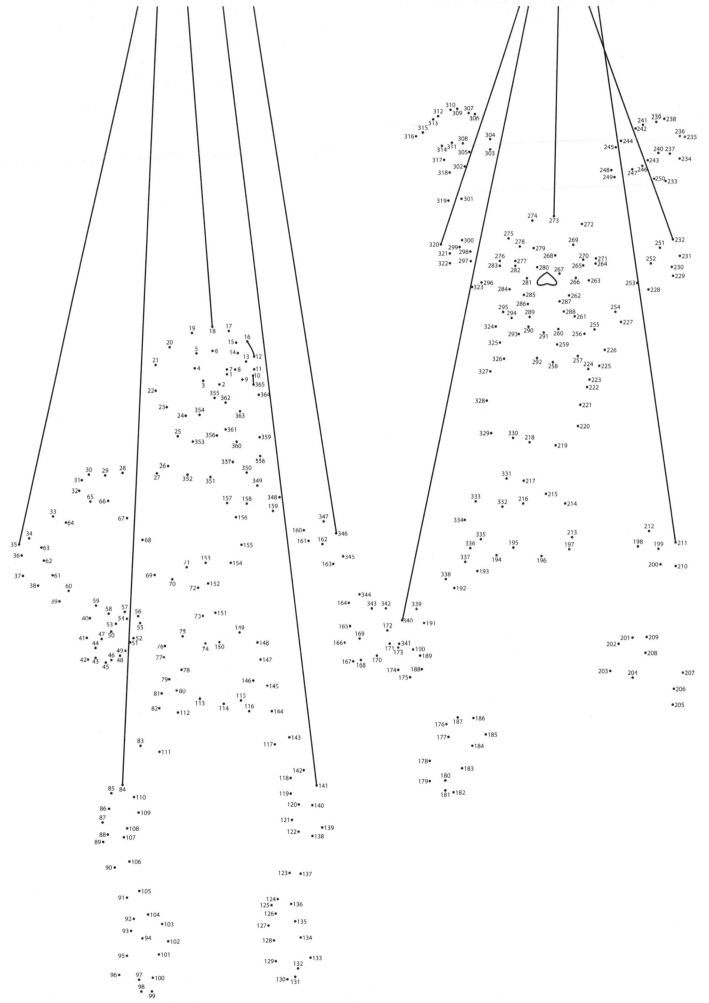

53

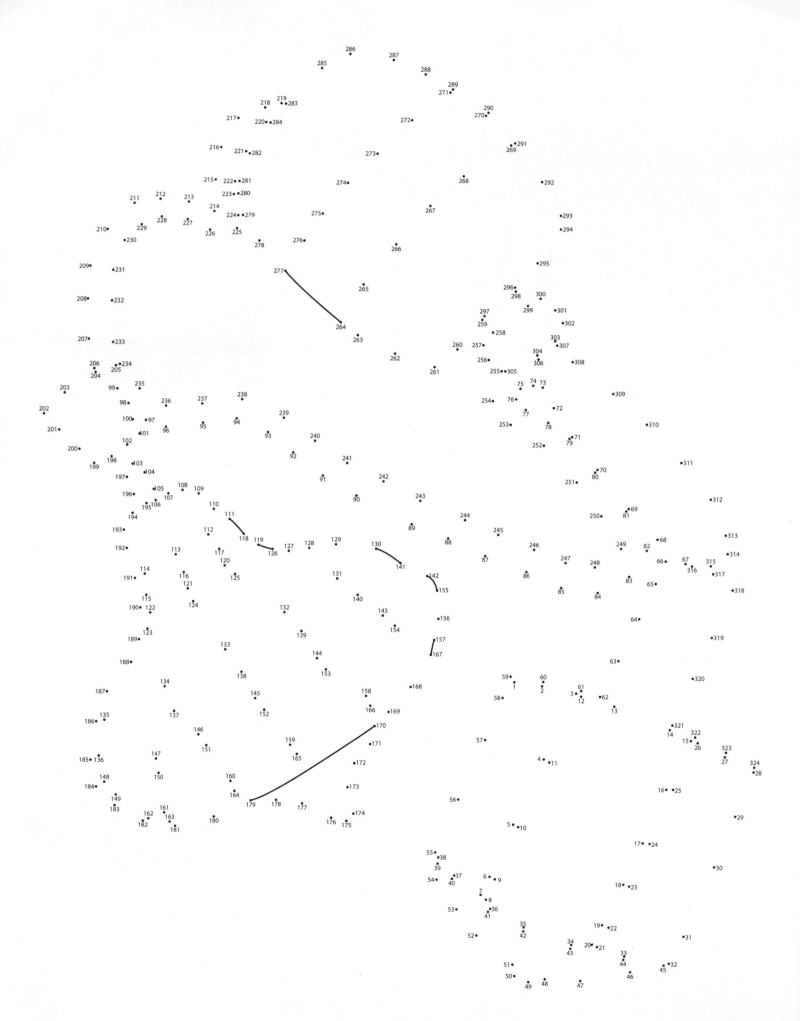

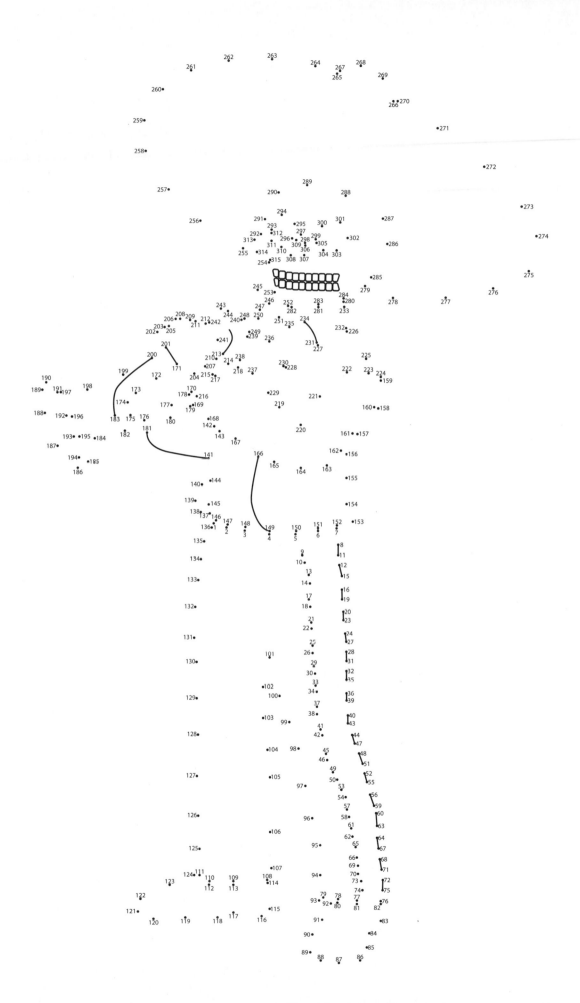

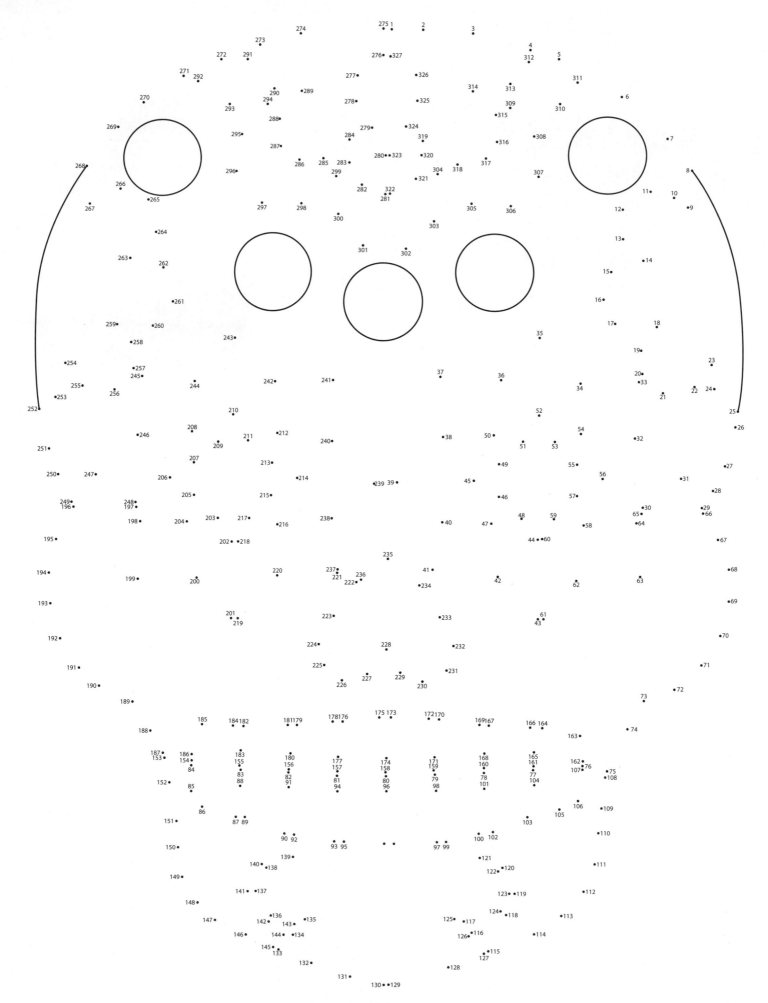

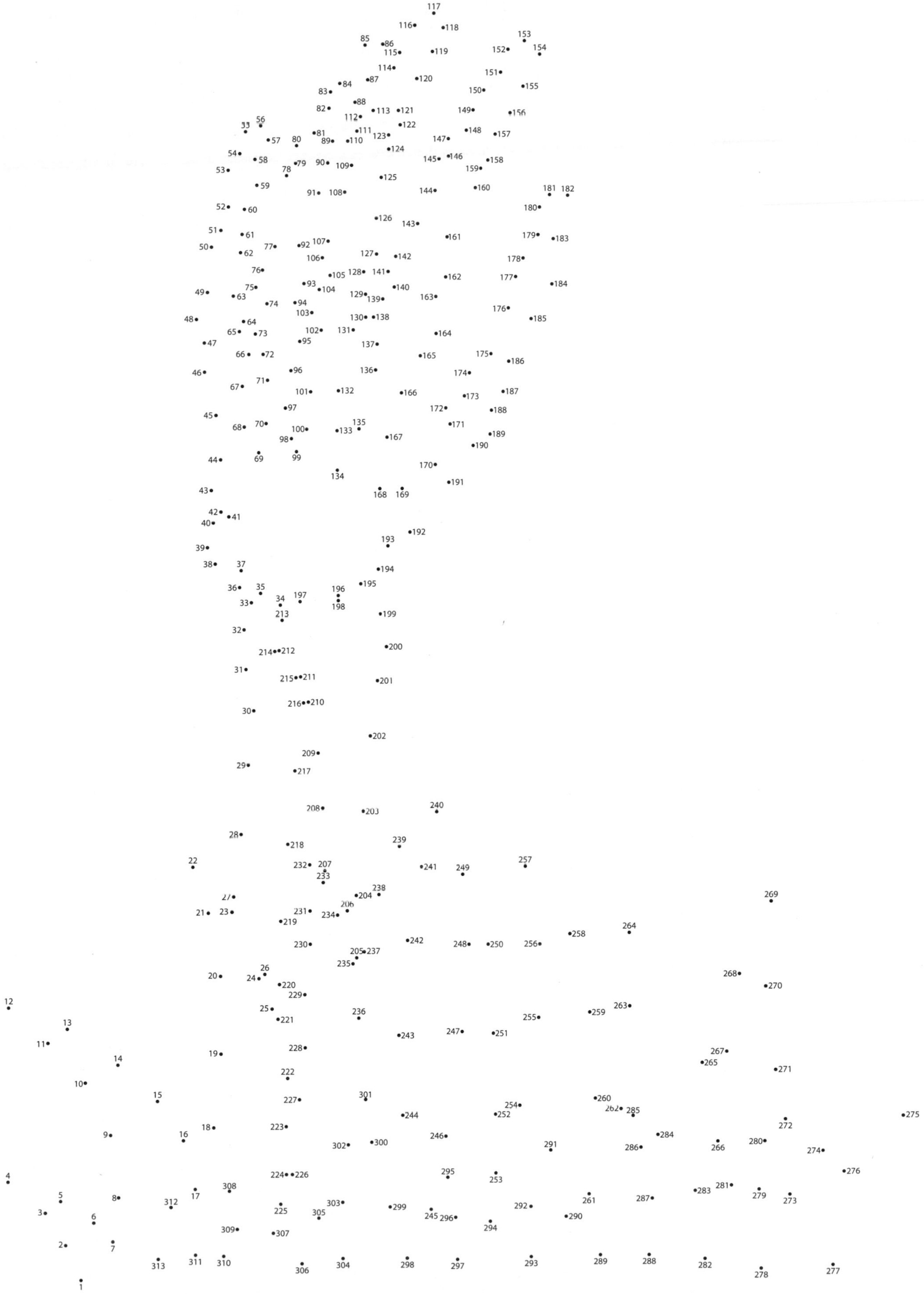

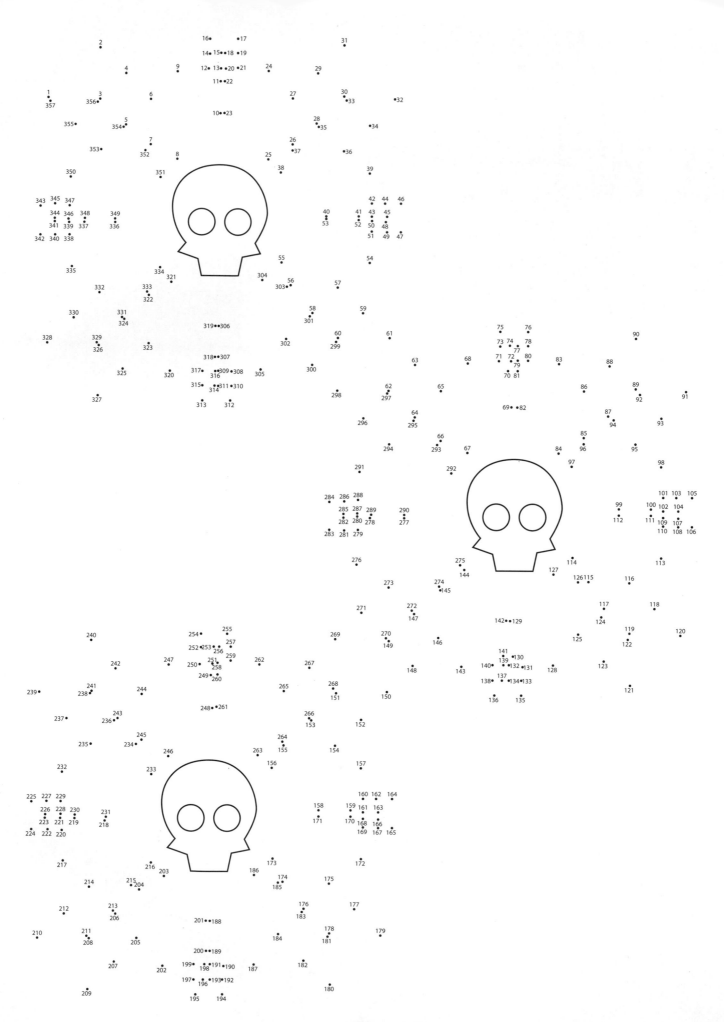

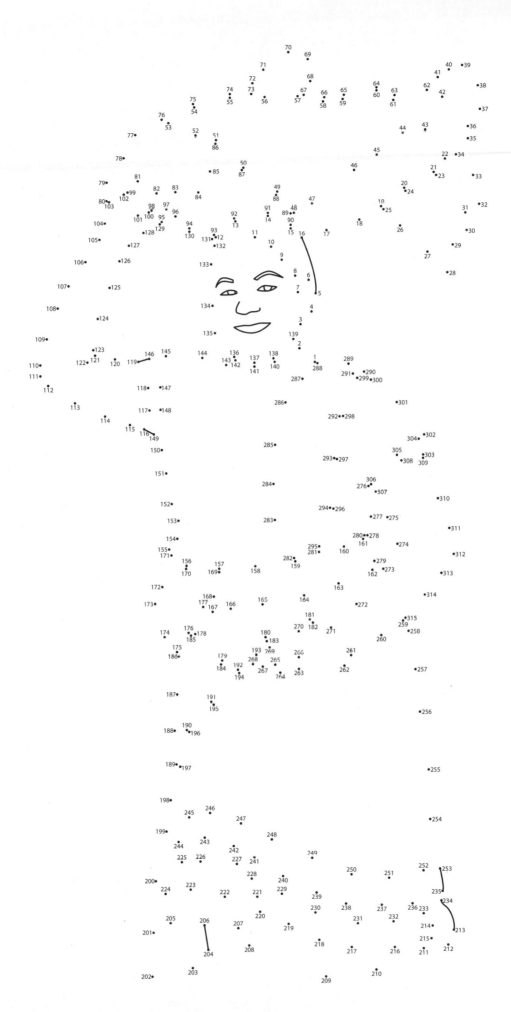

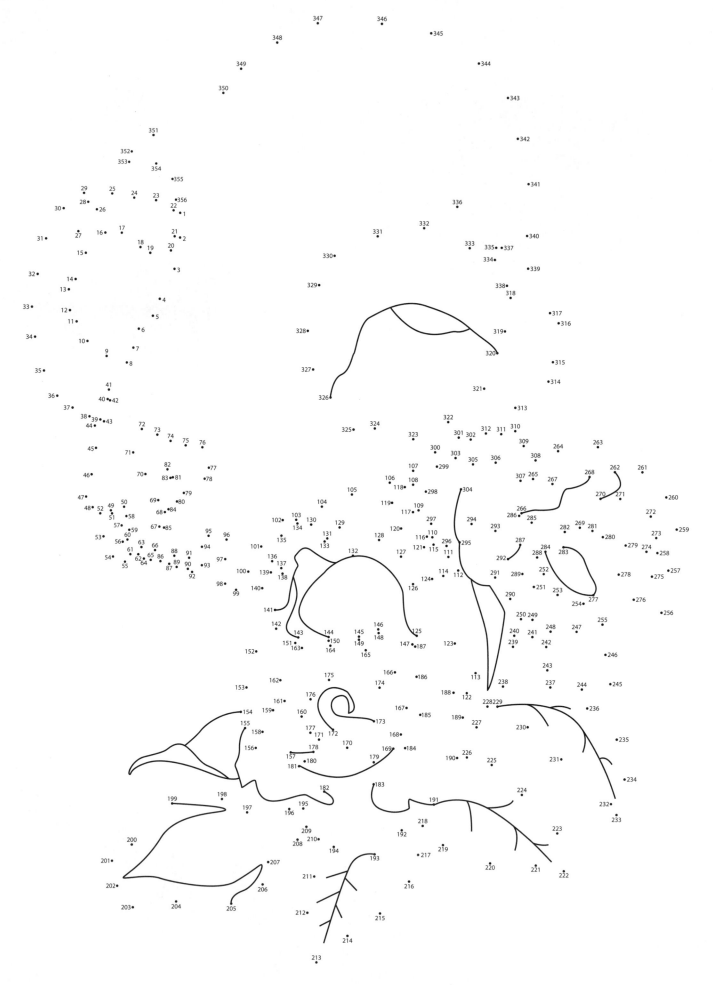

60

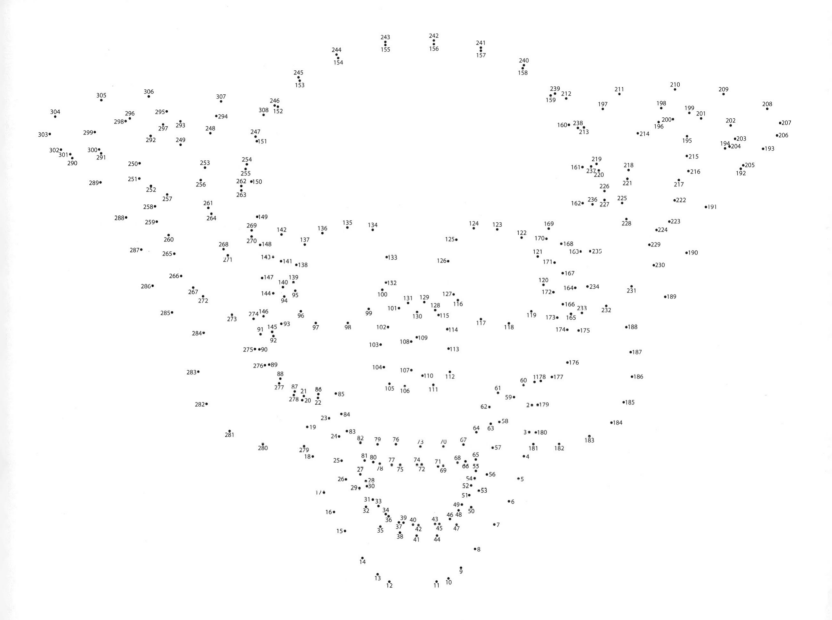

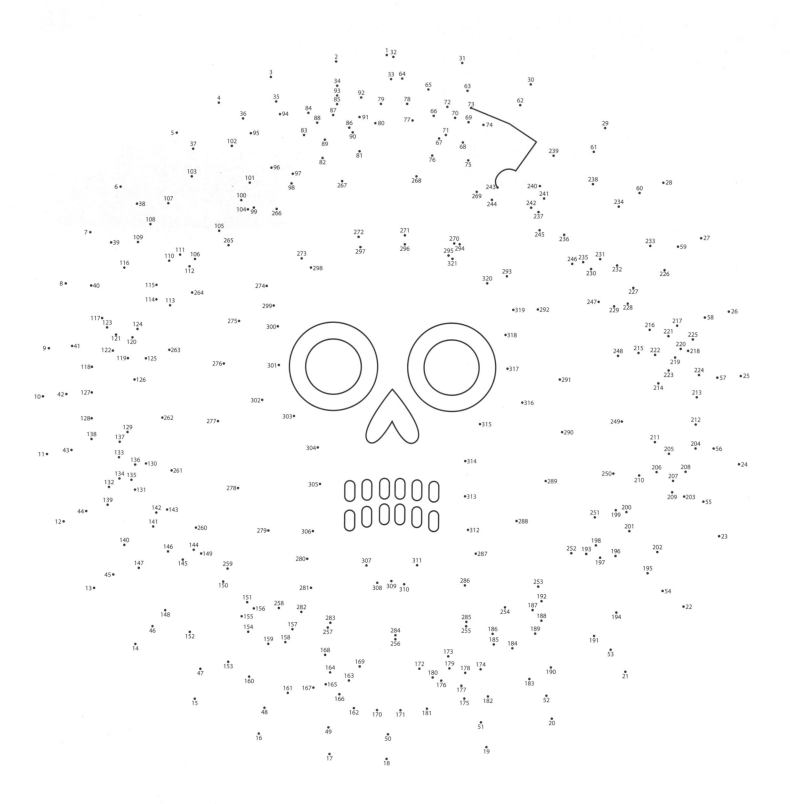

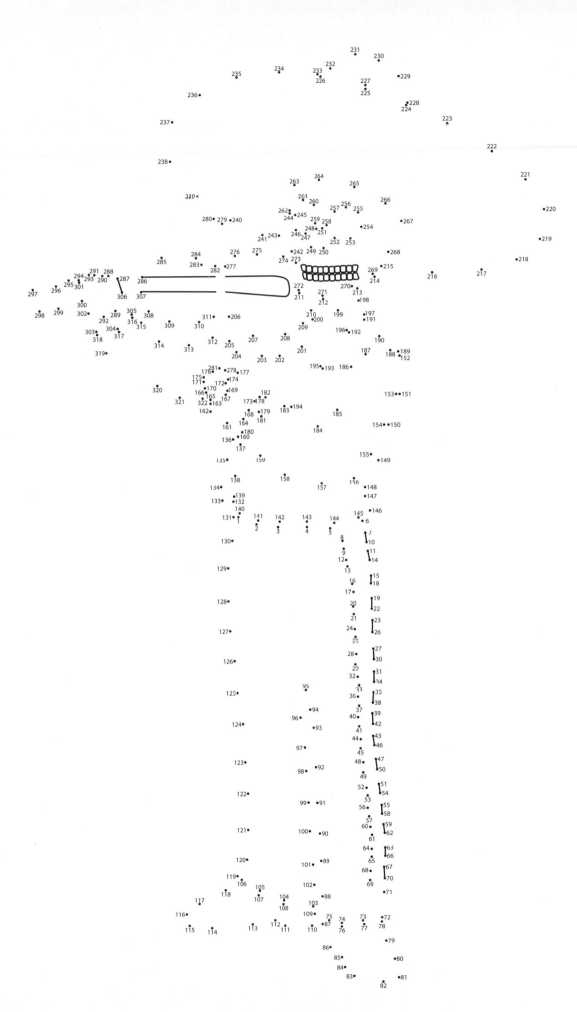

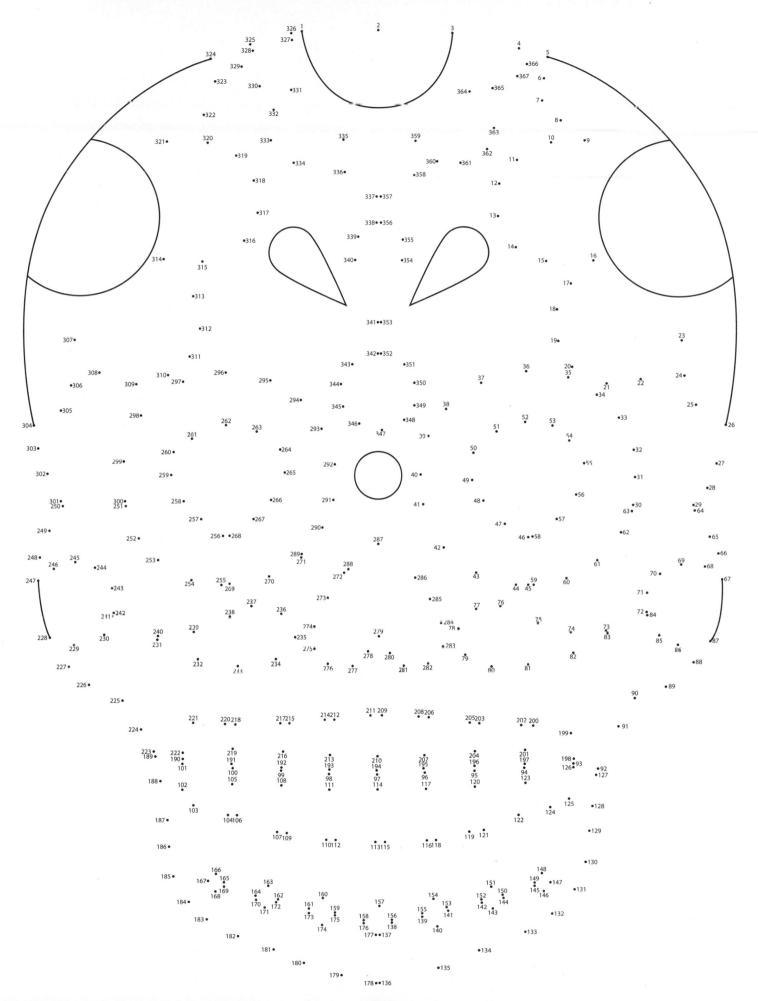

68

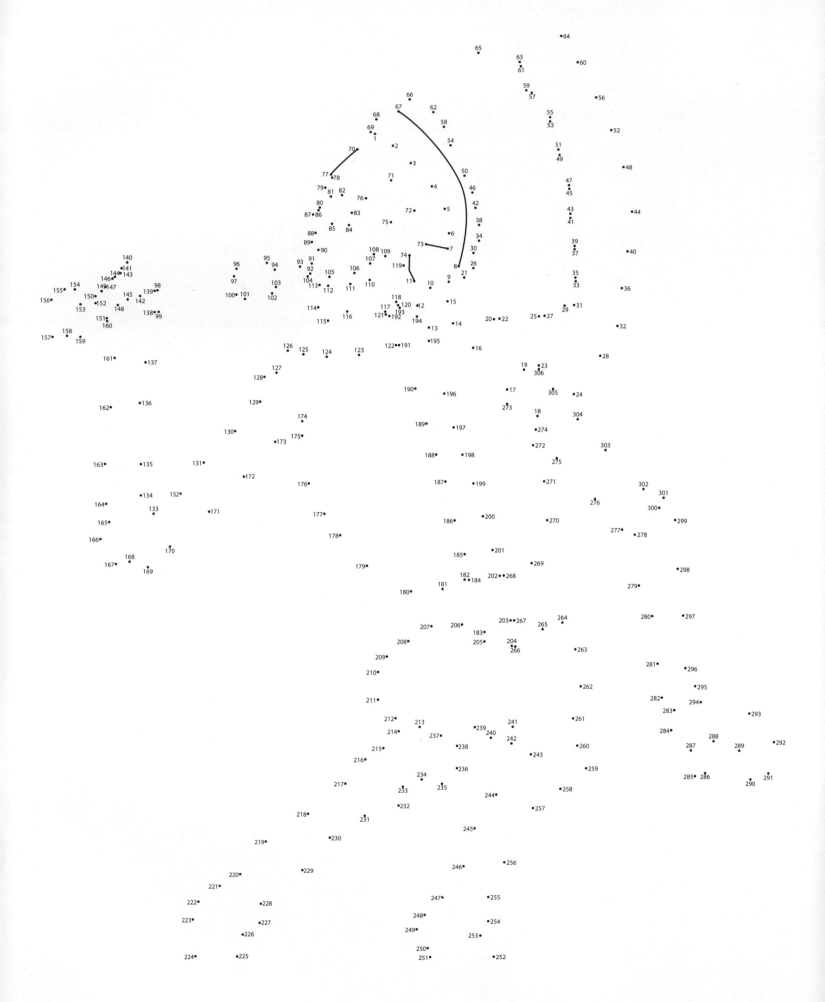

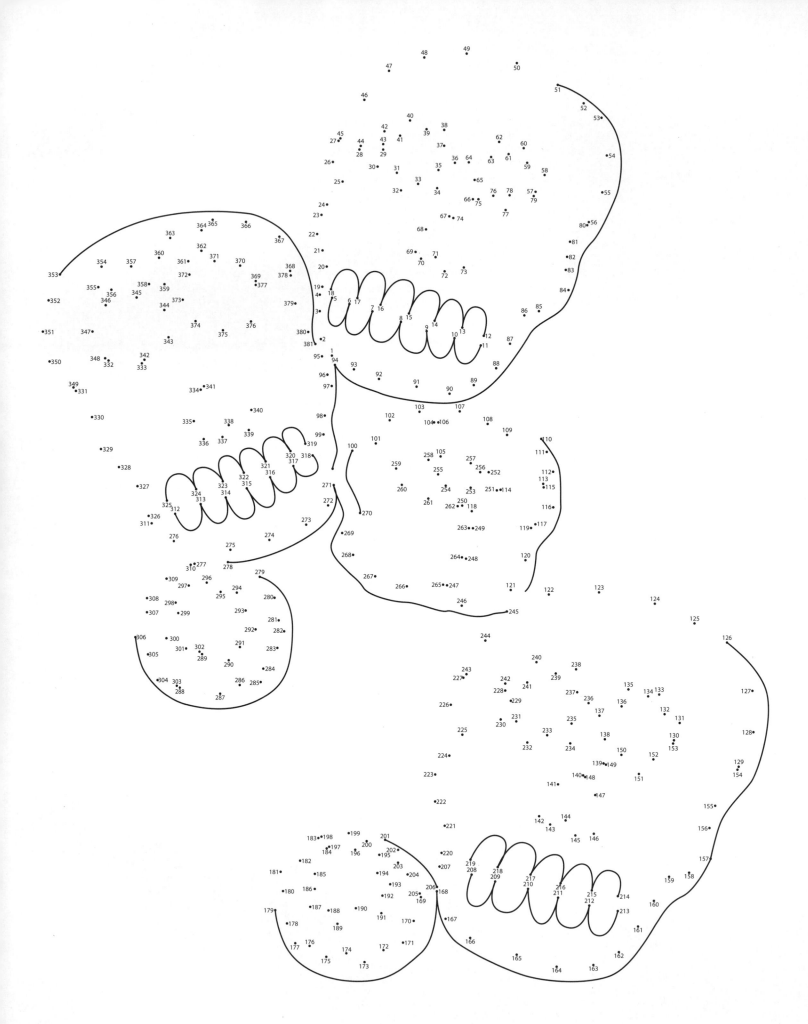

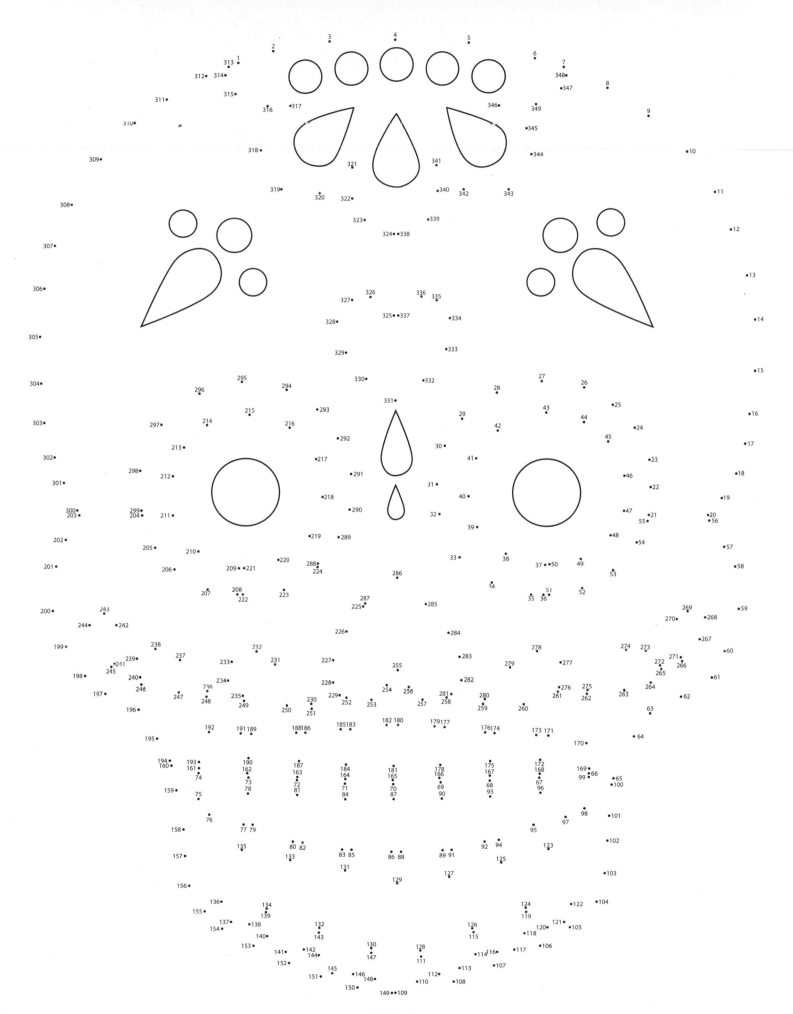

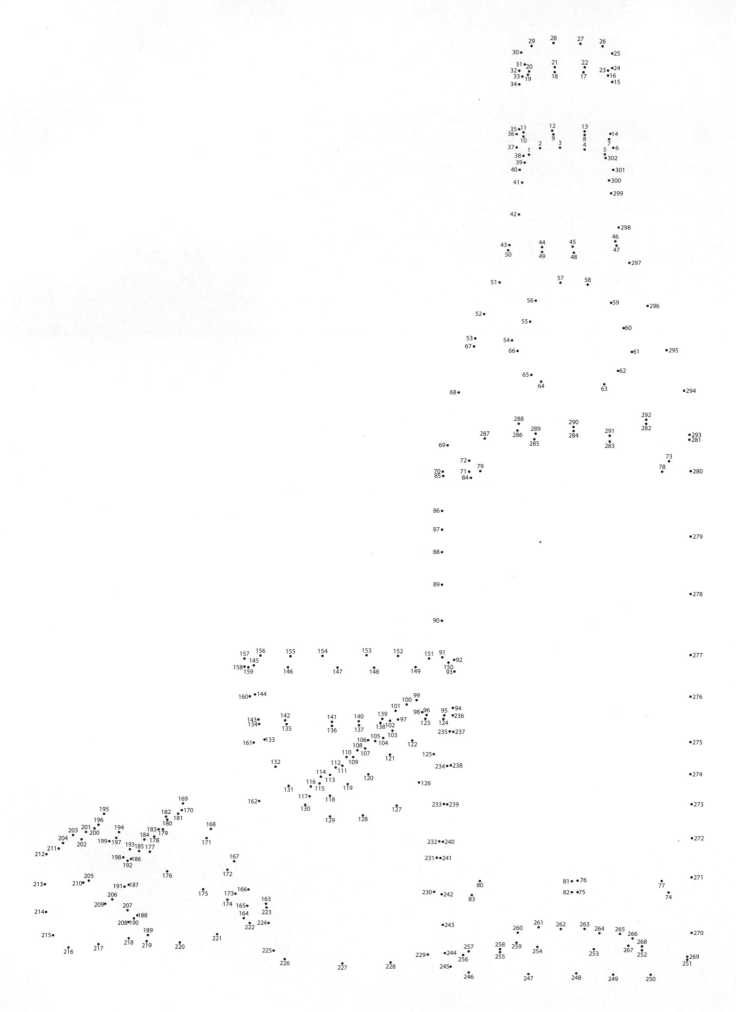

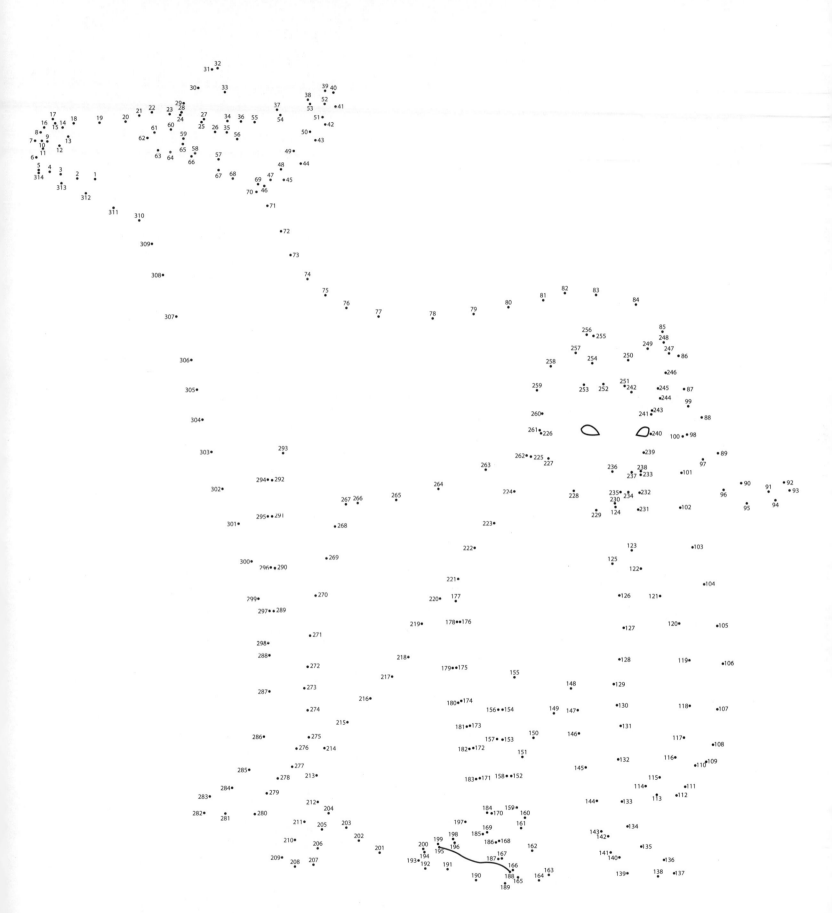

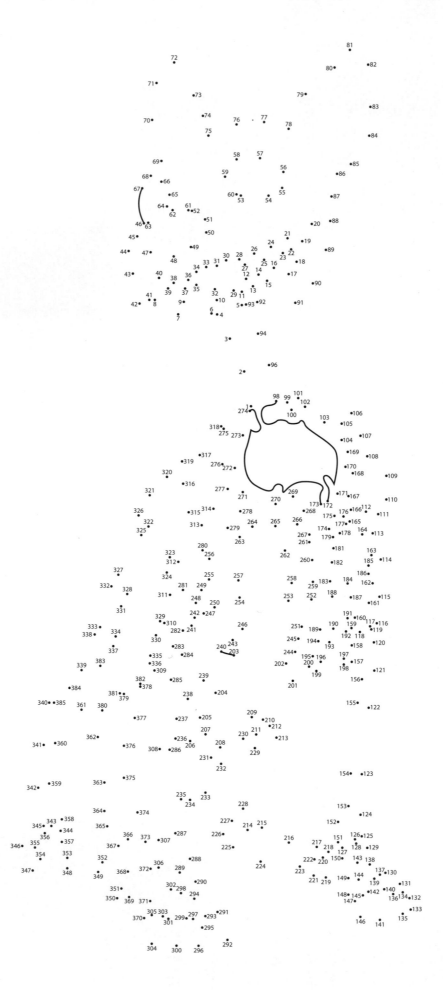

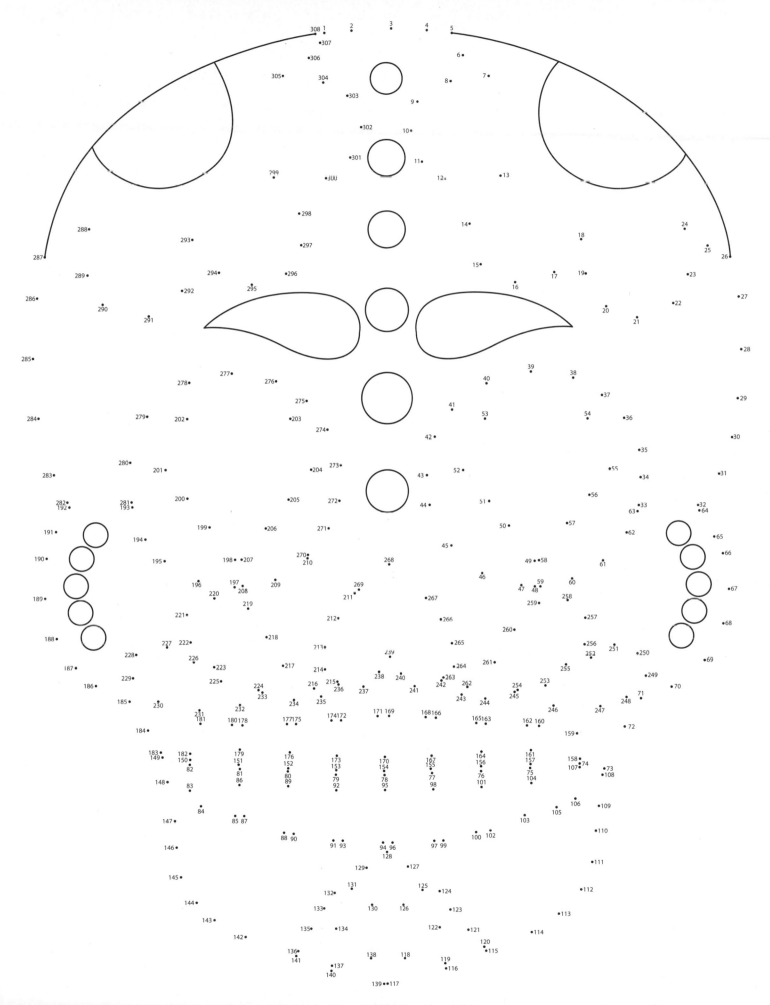

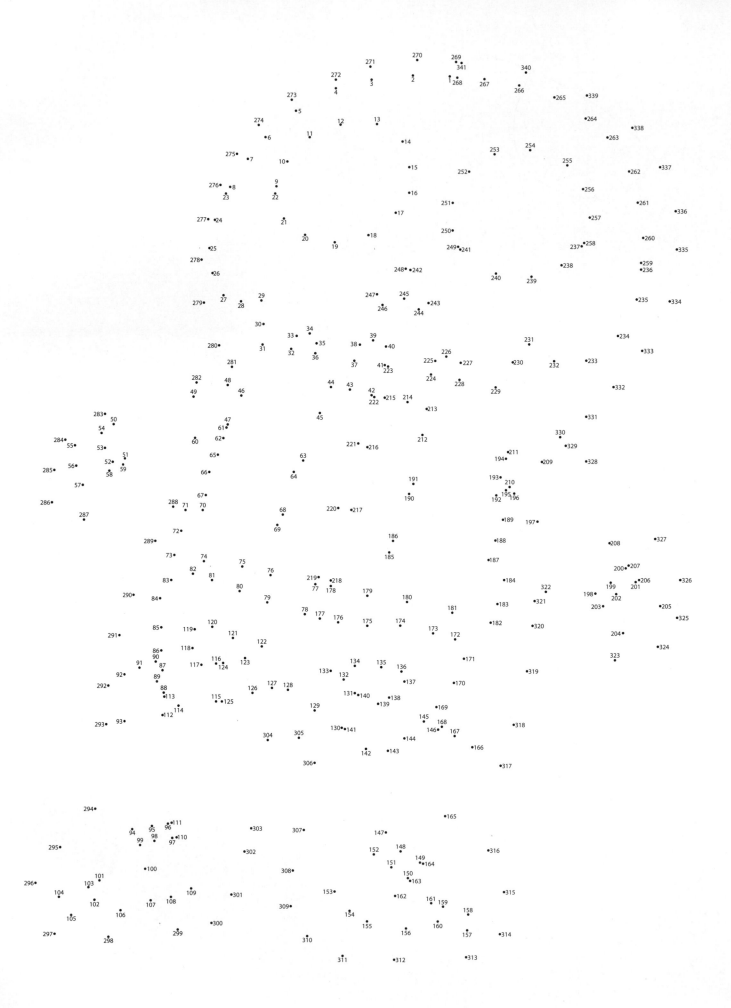

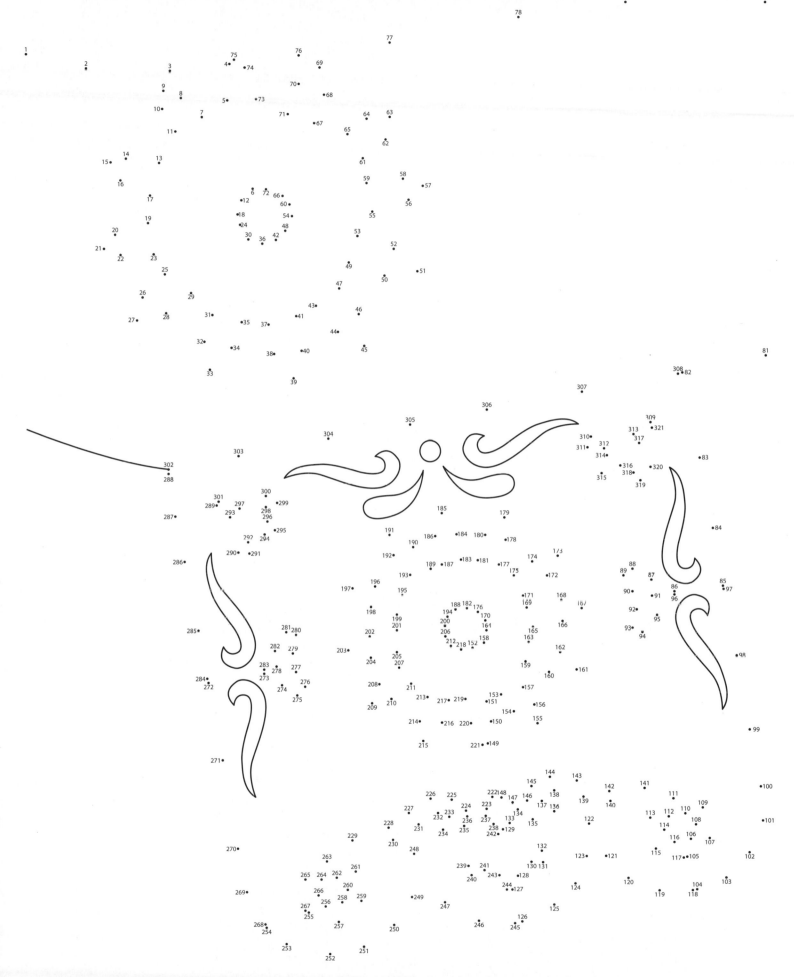

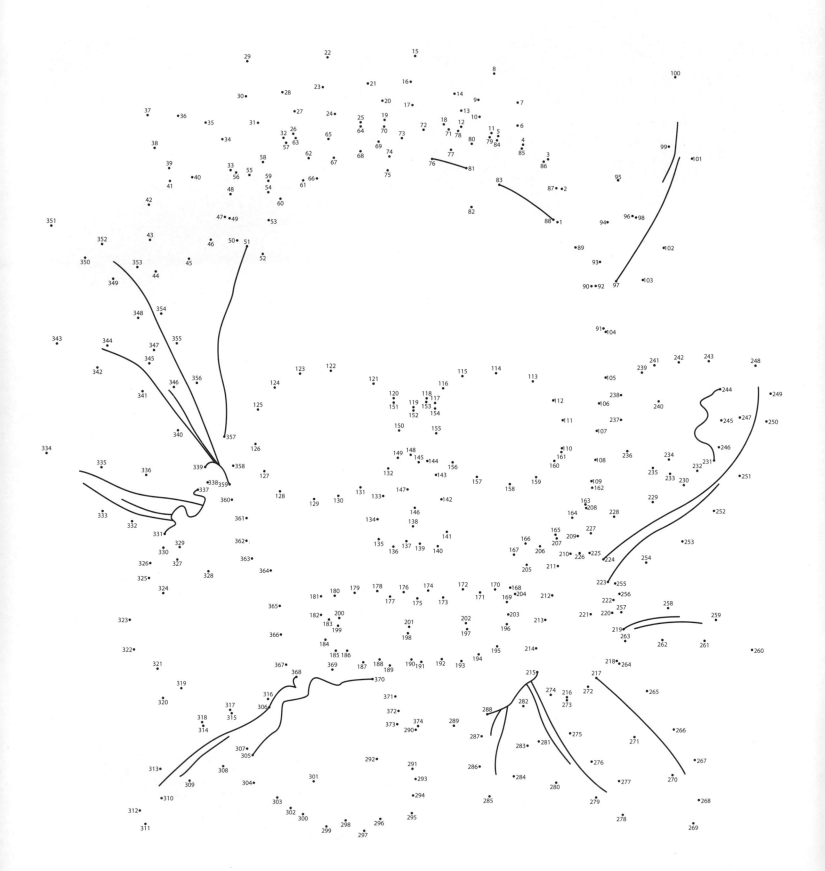

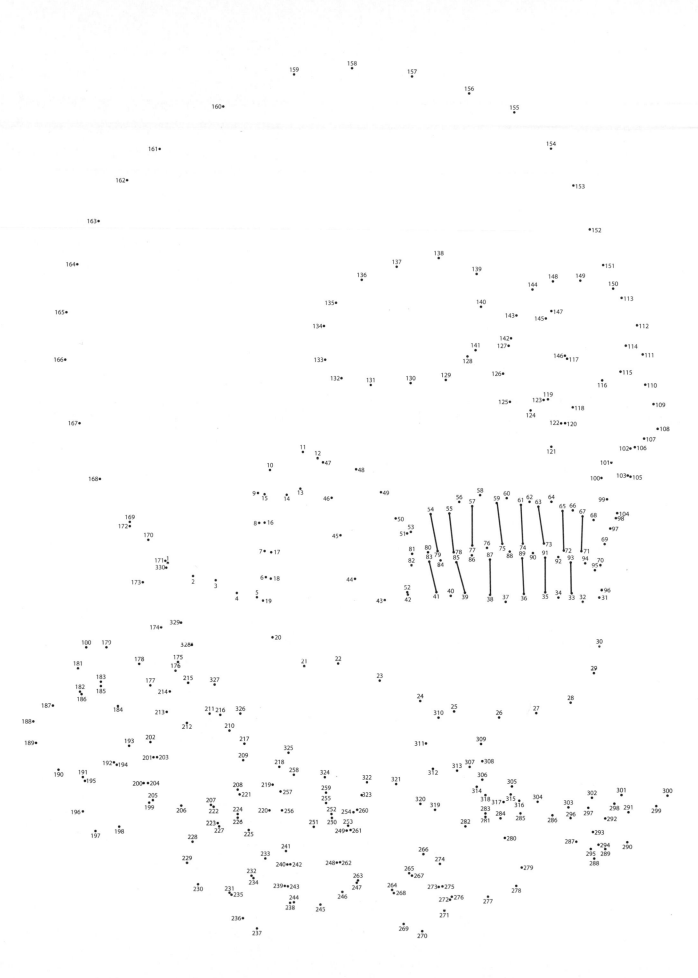

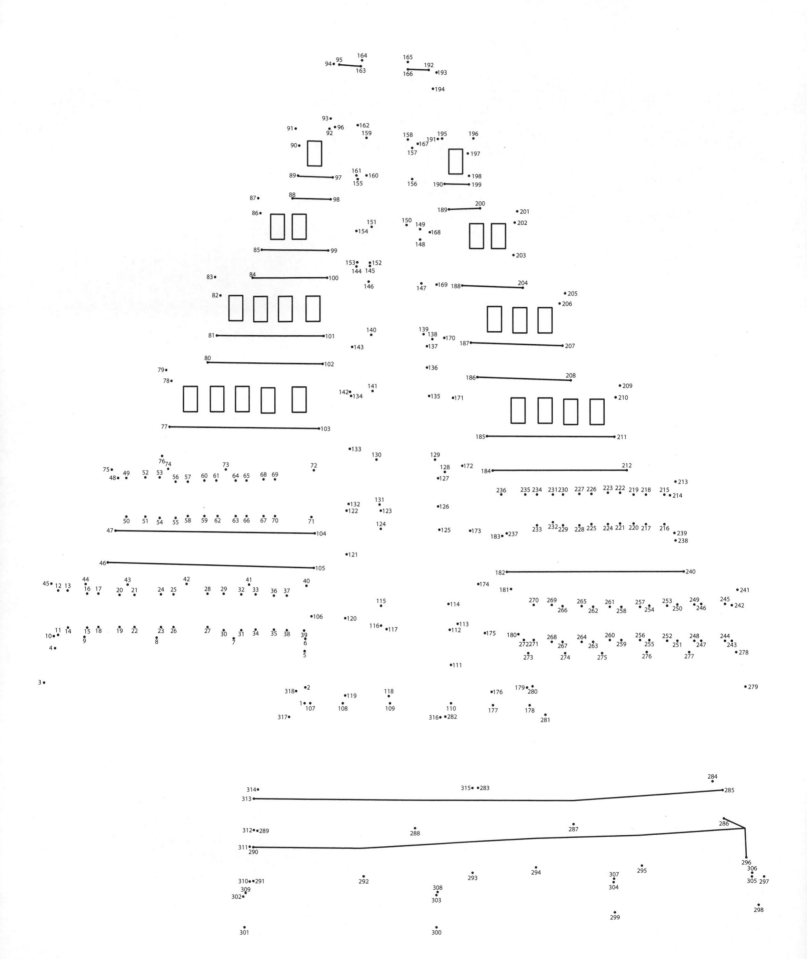

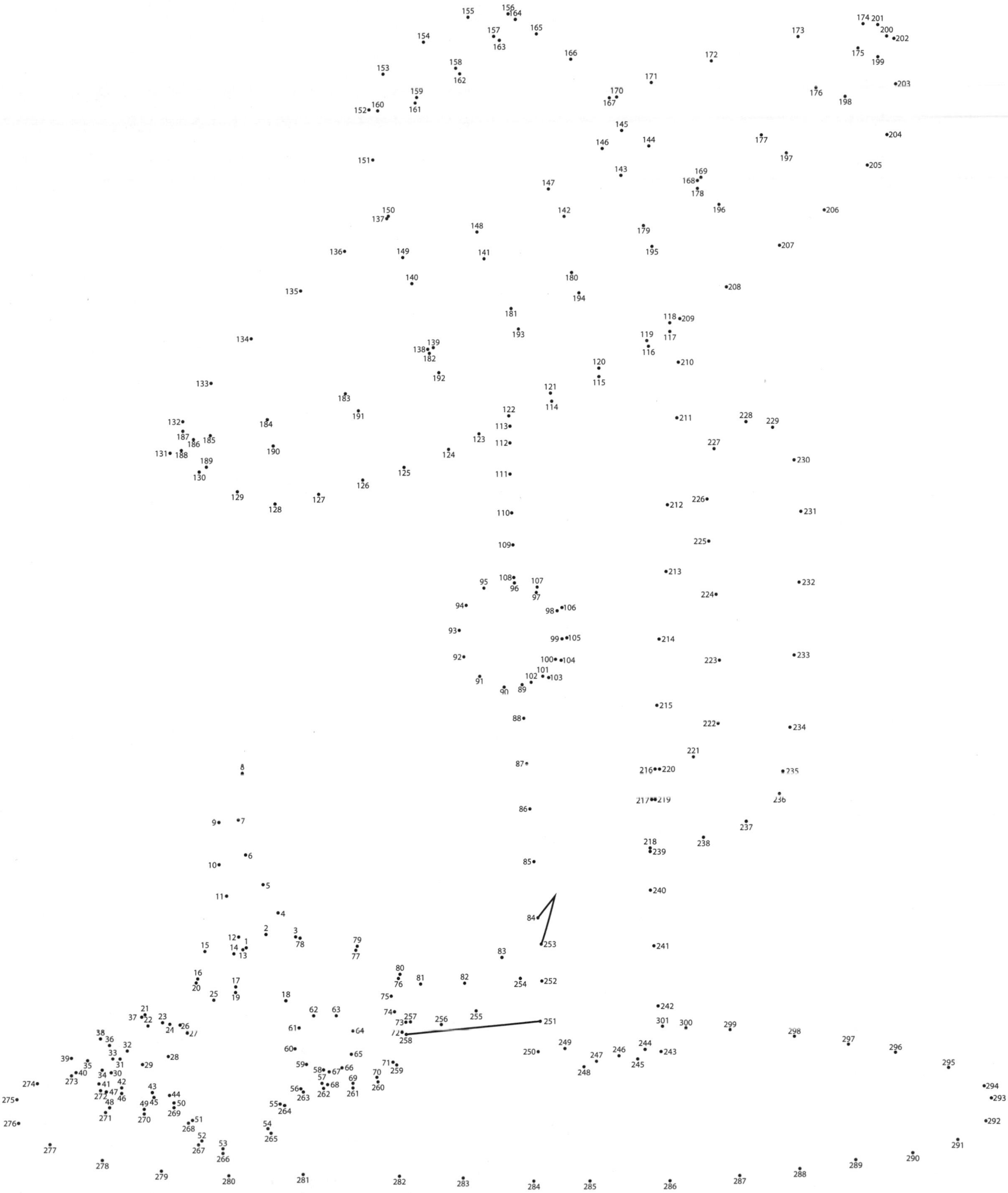

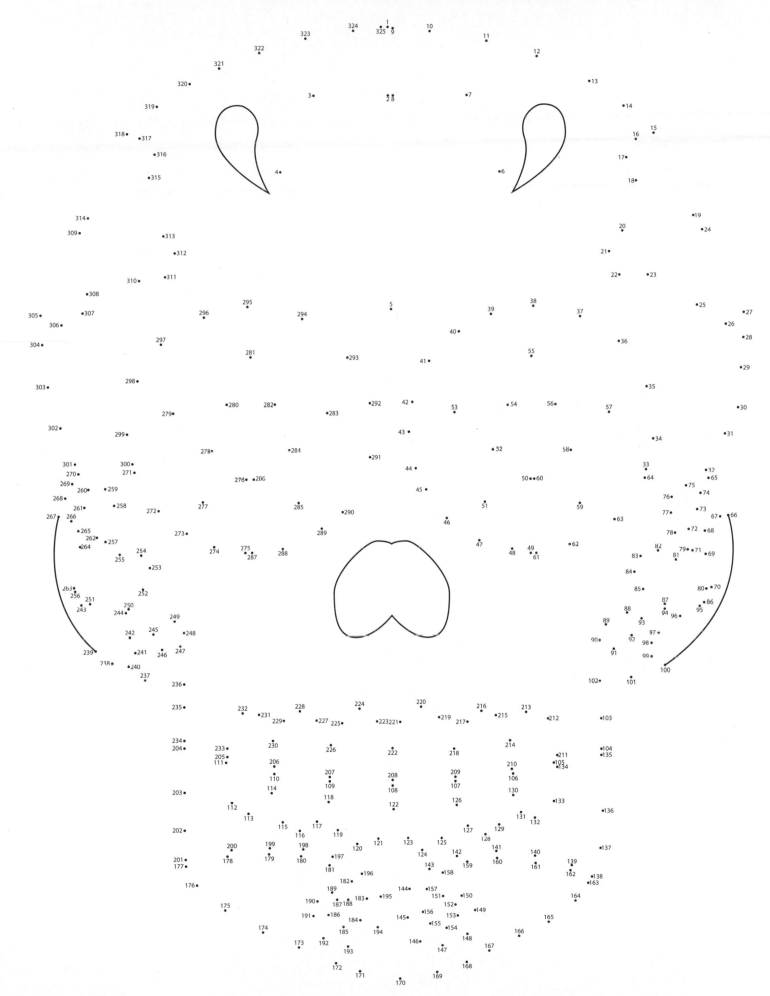

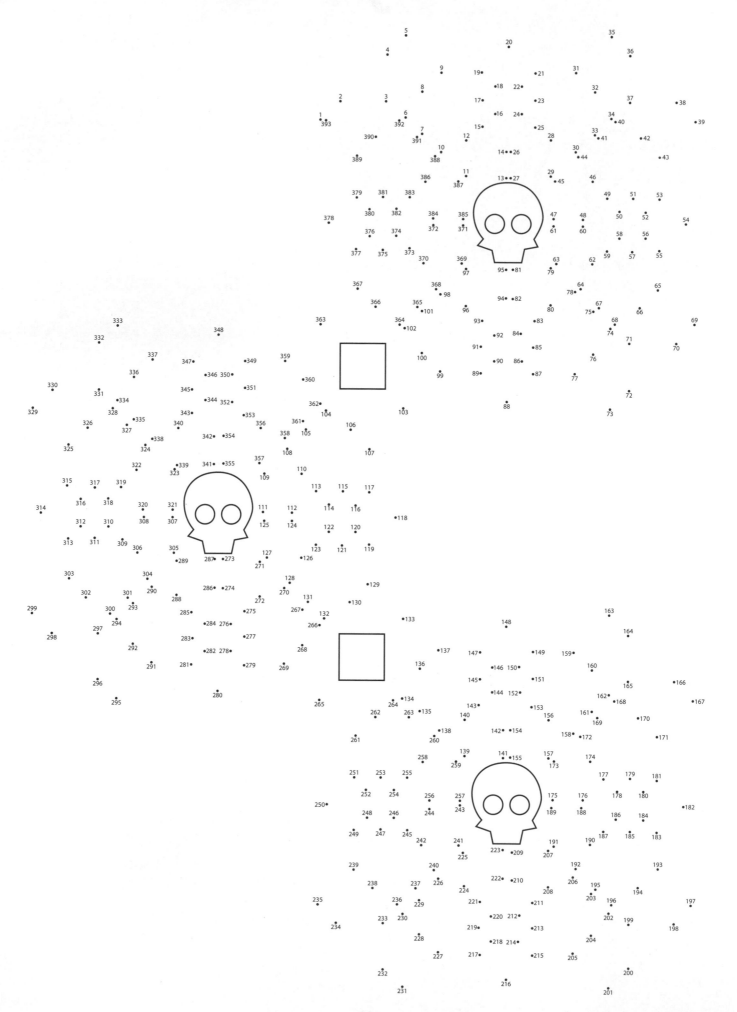

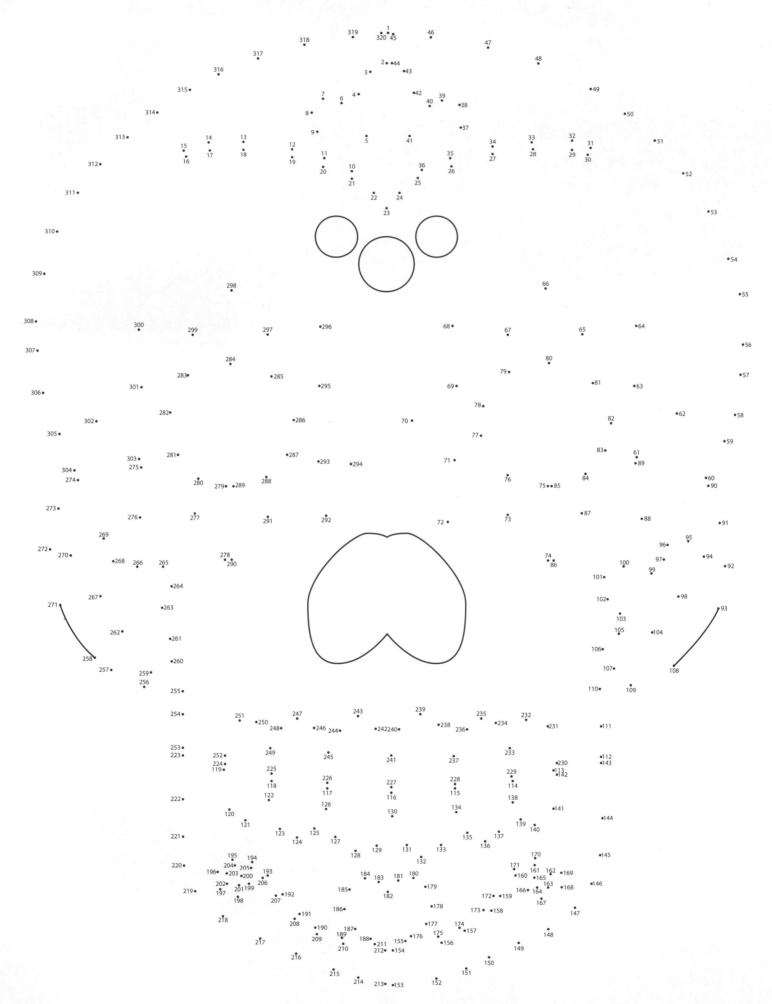

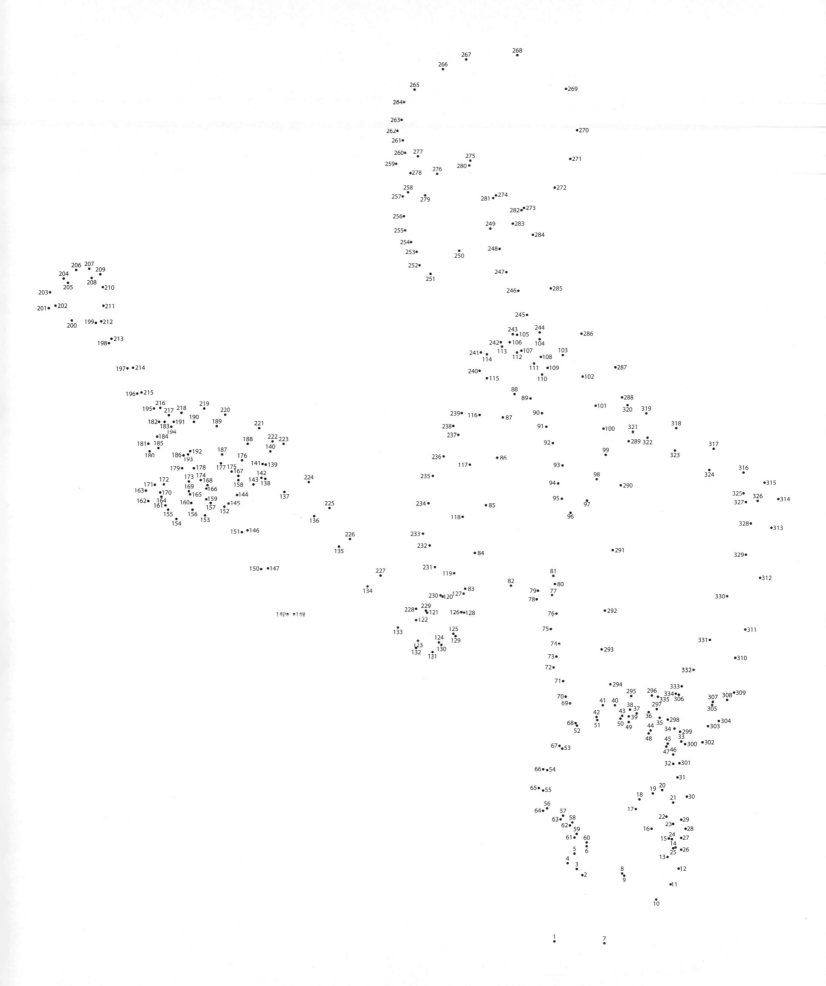

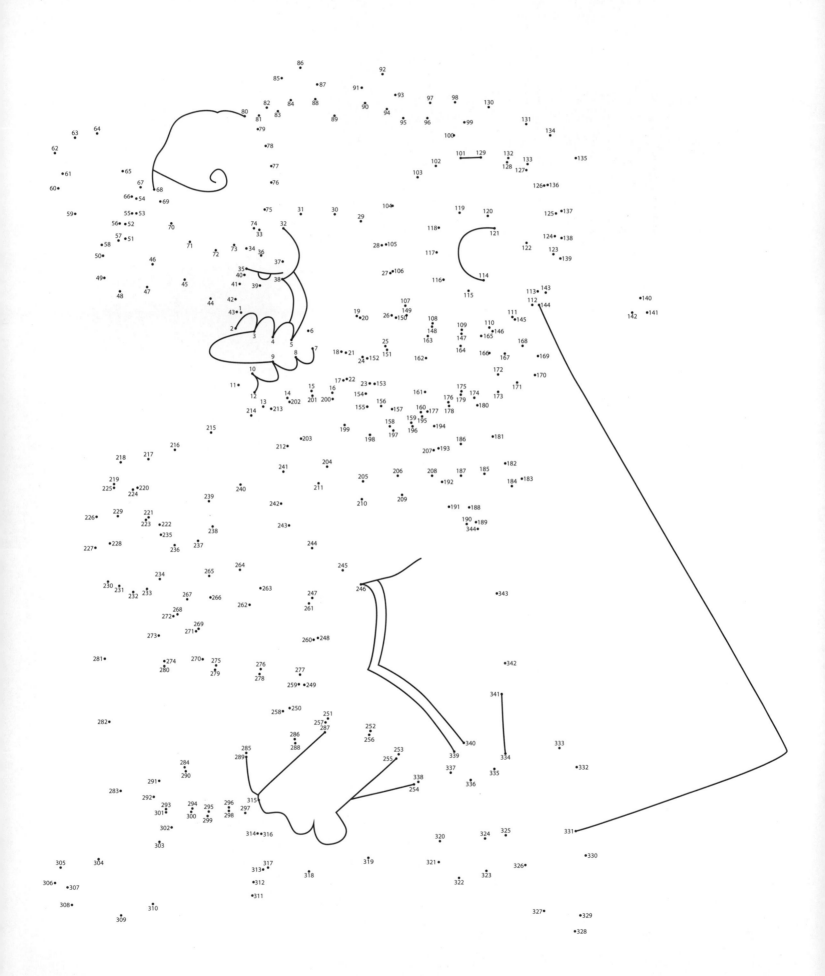

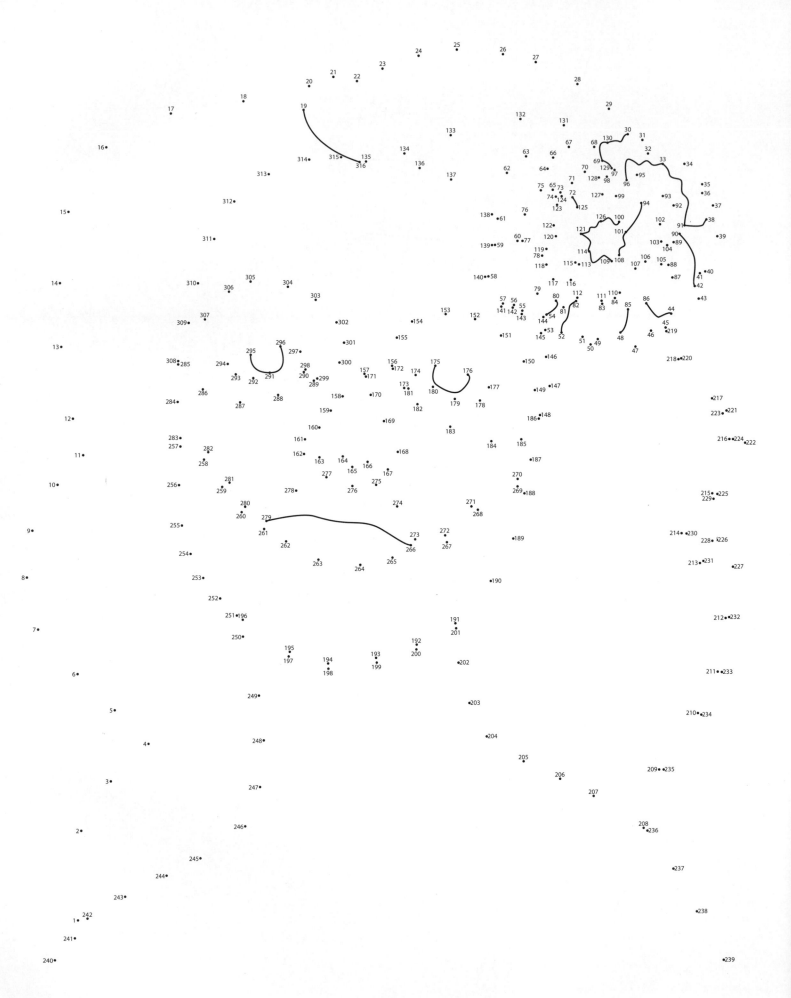

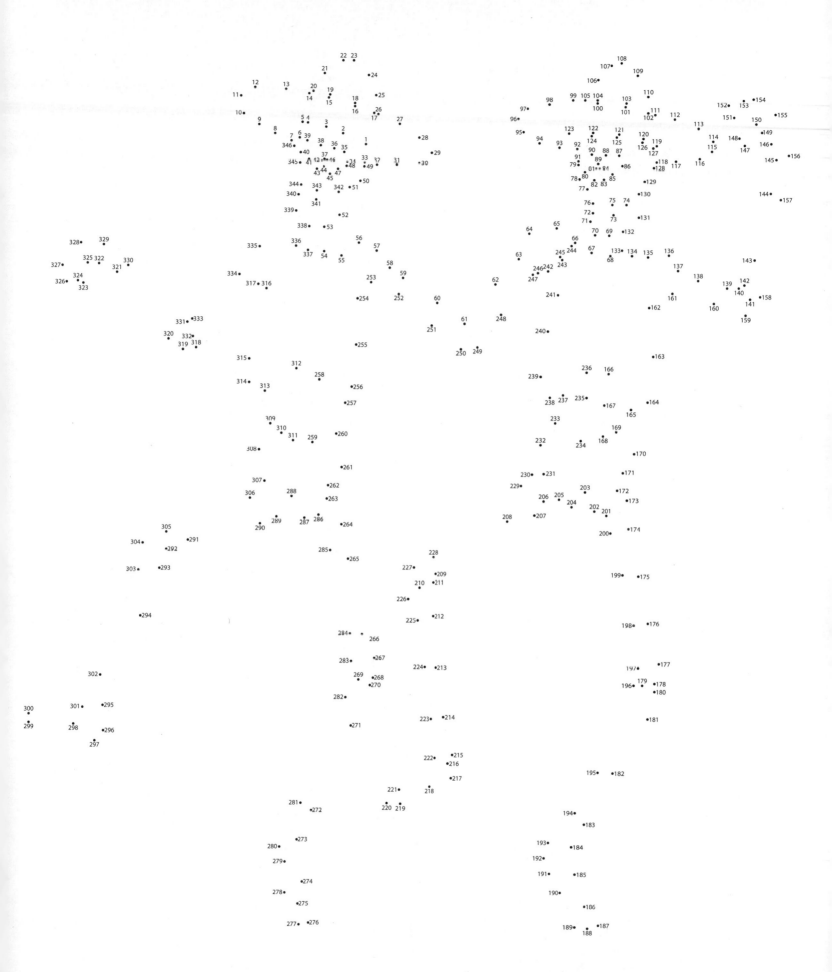

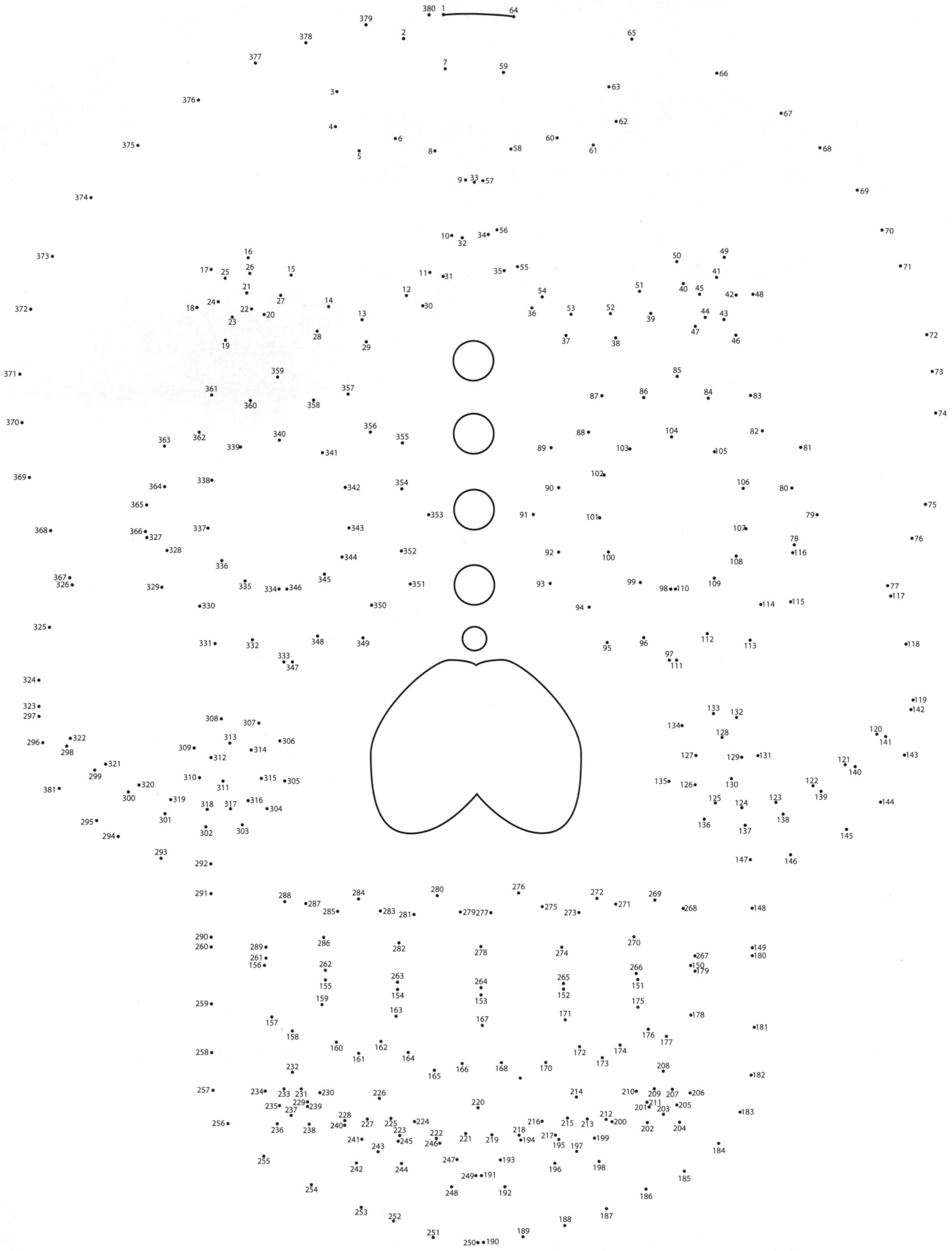

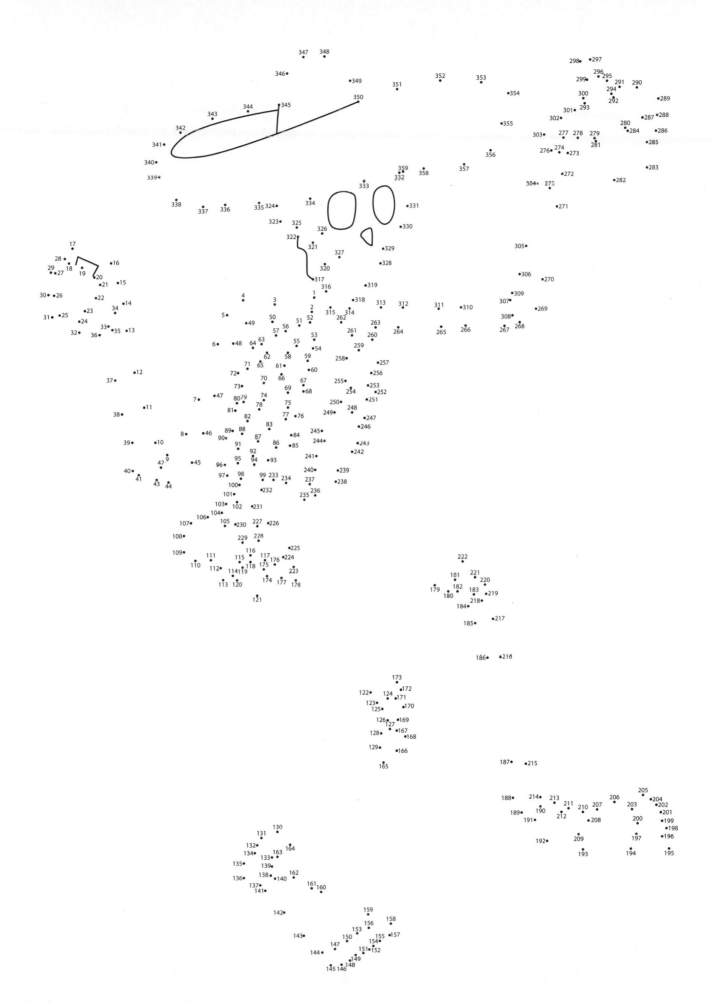

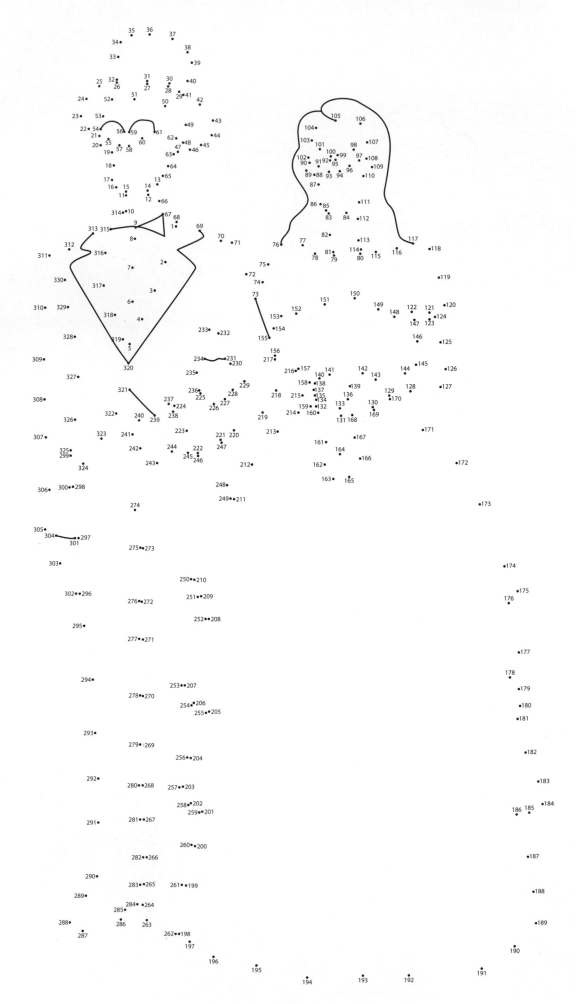

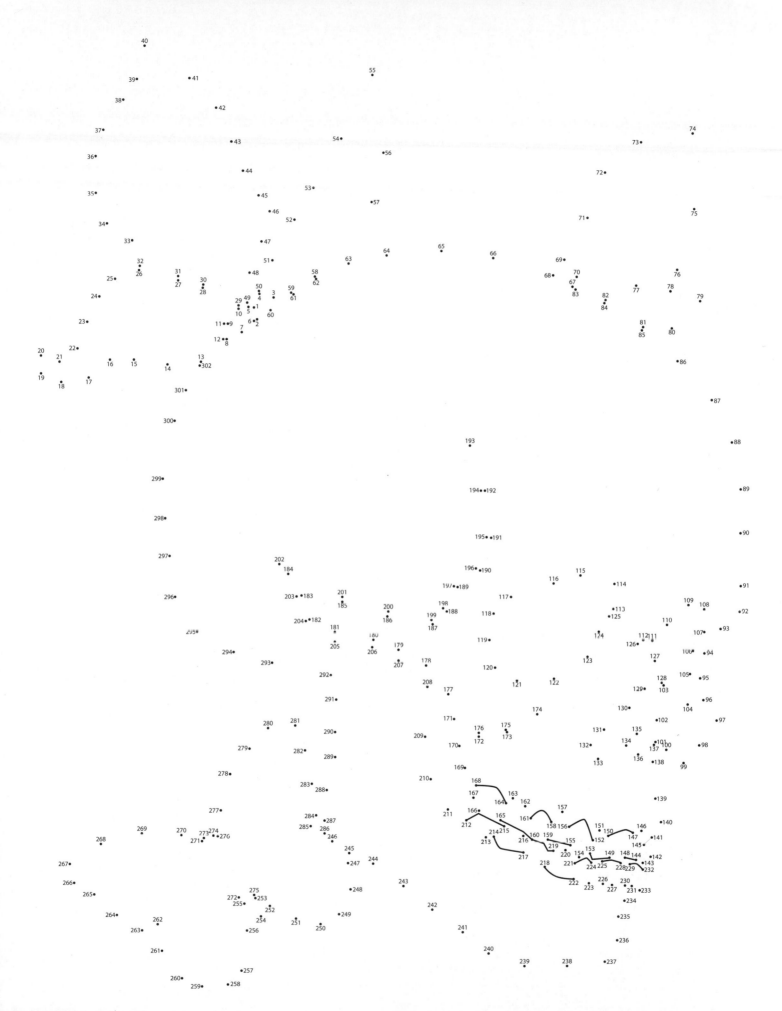

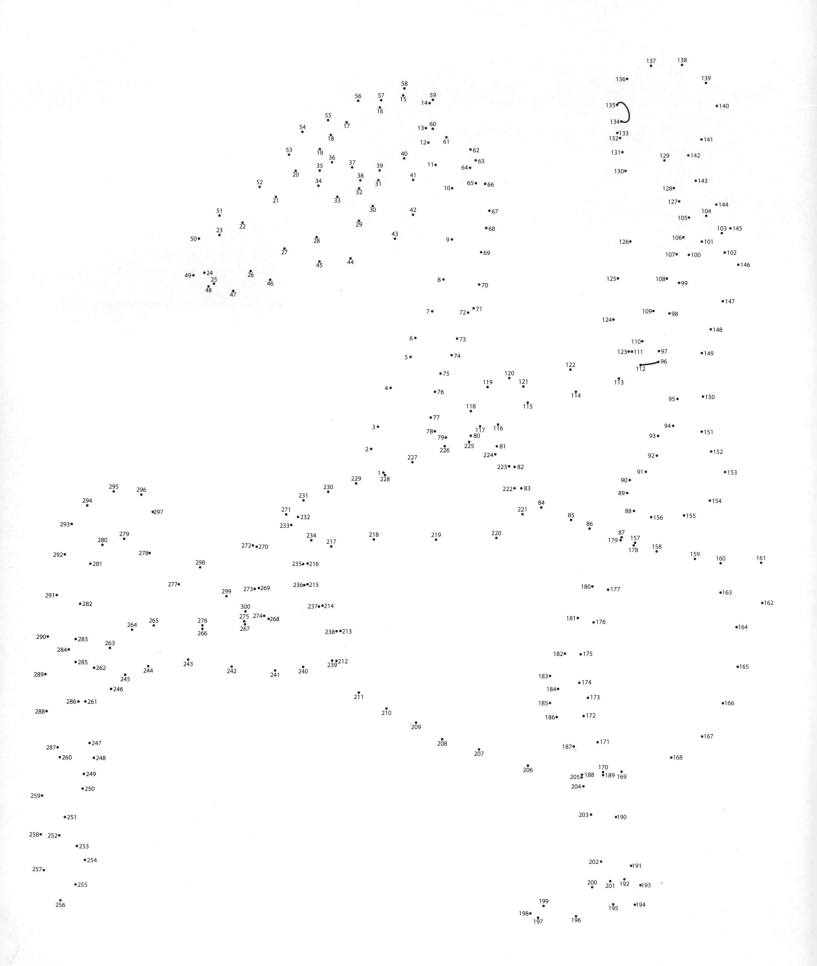

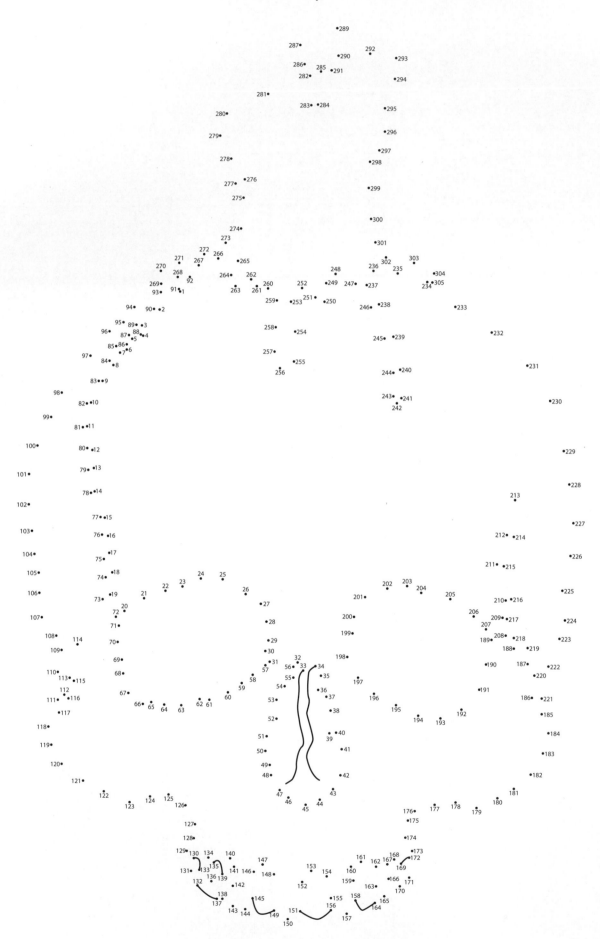

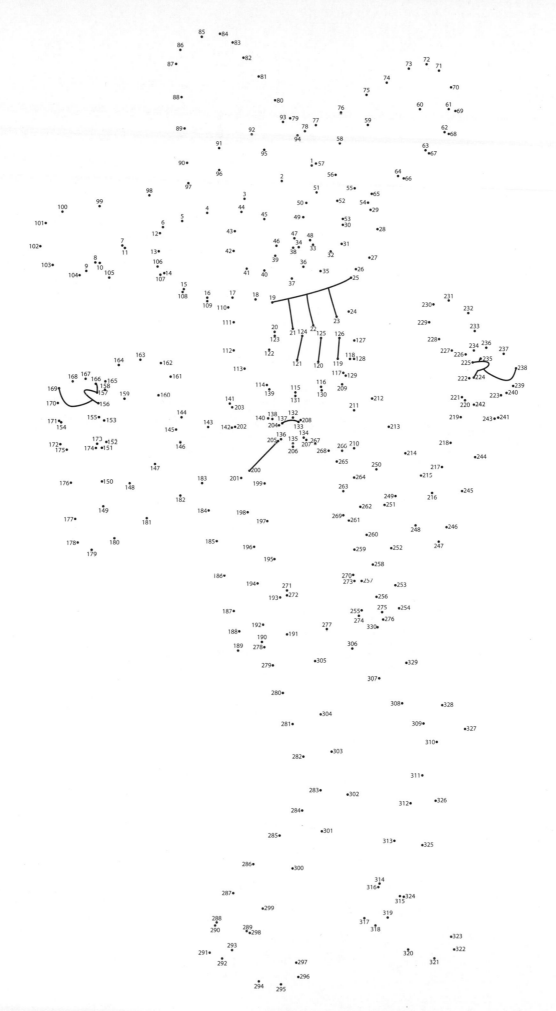

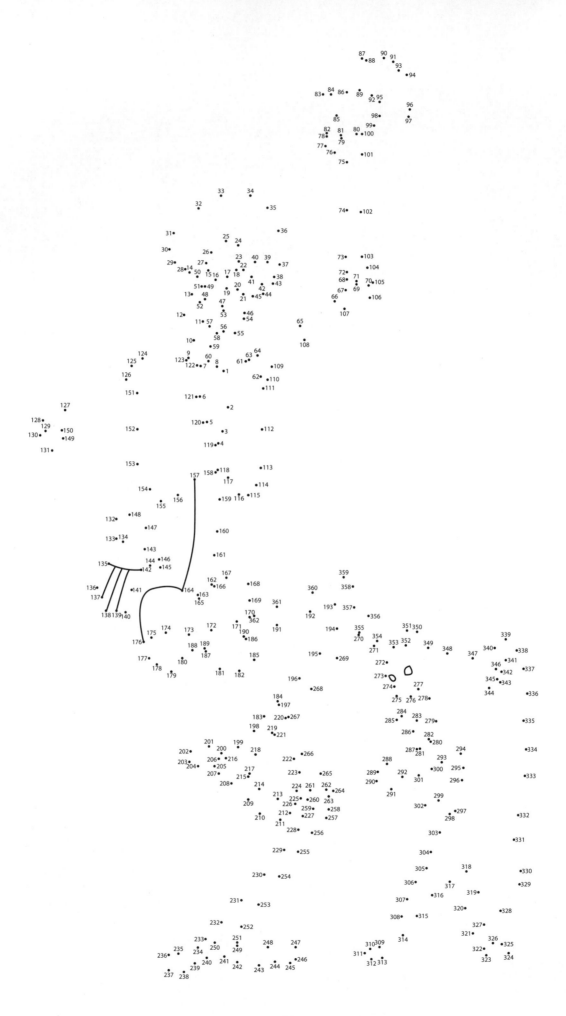

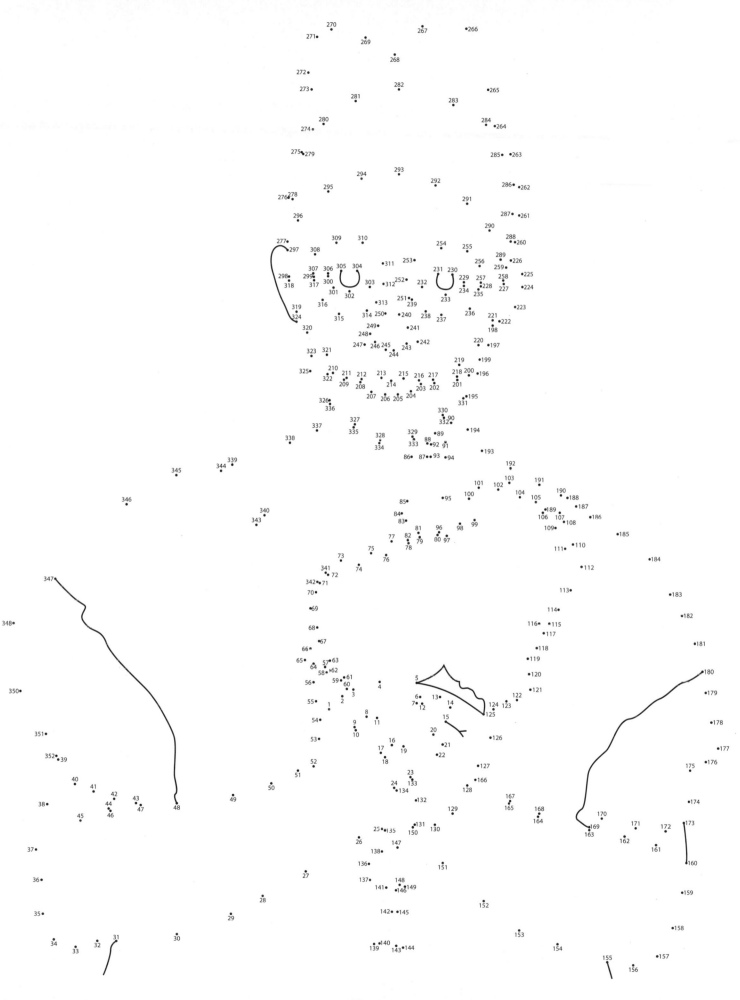

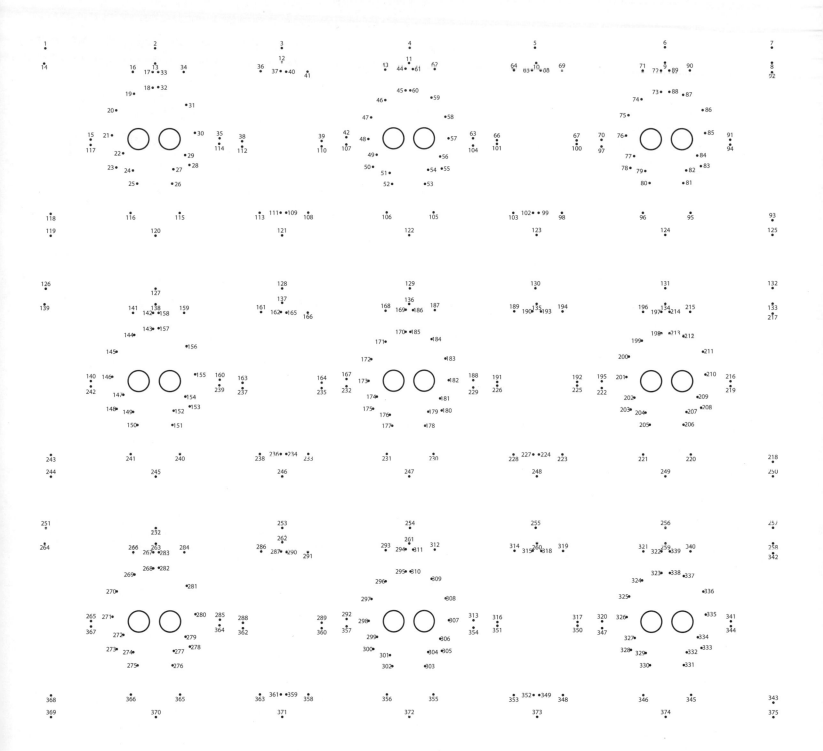

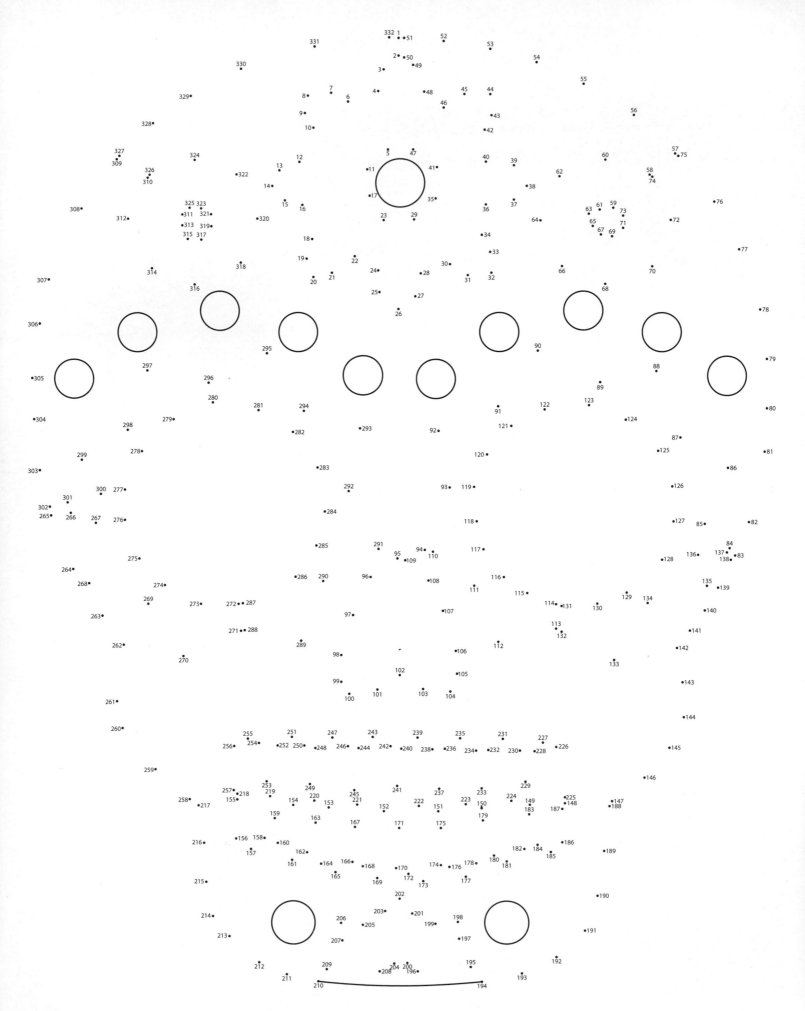

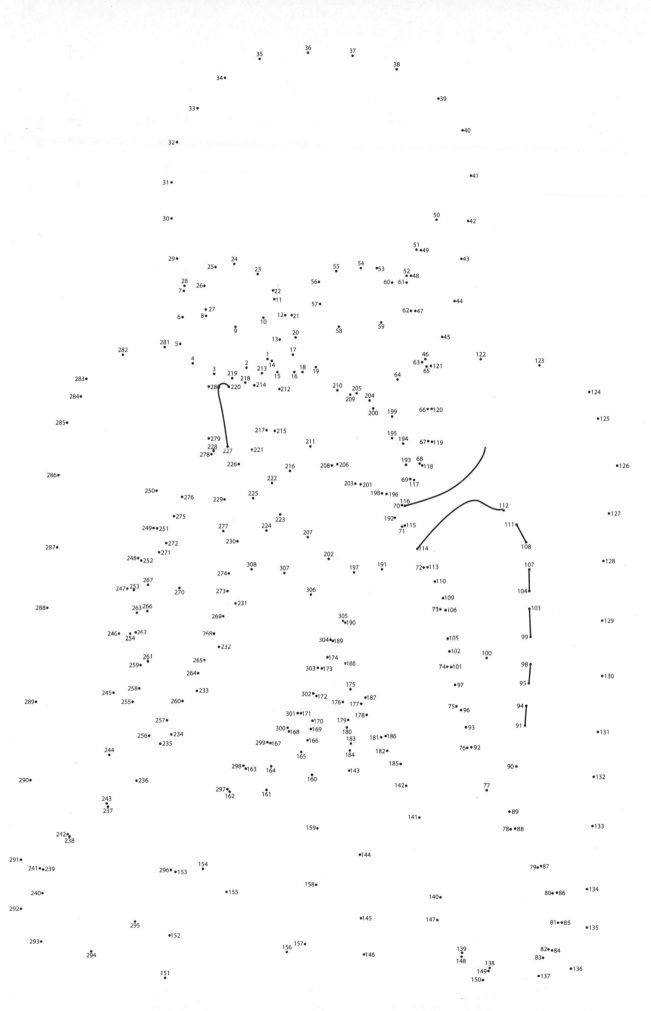

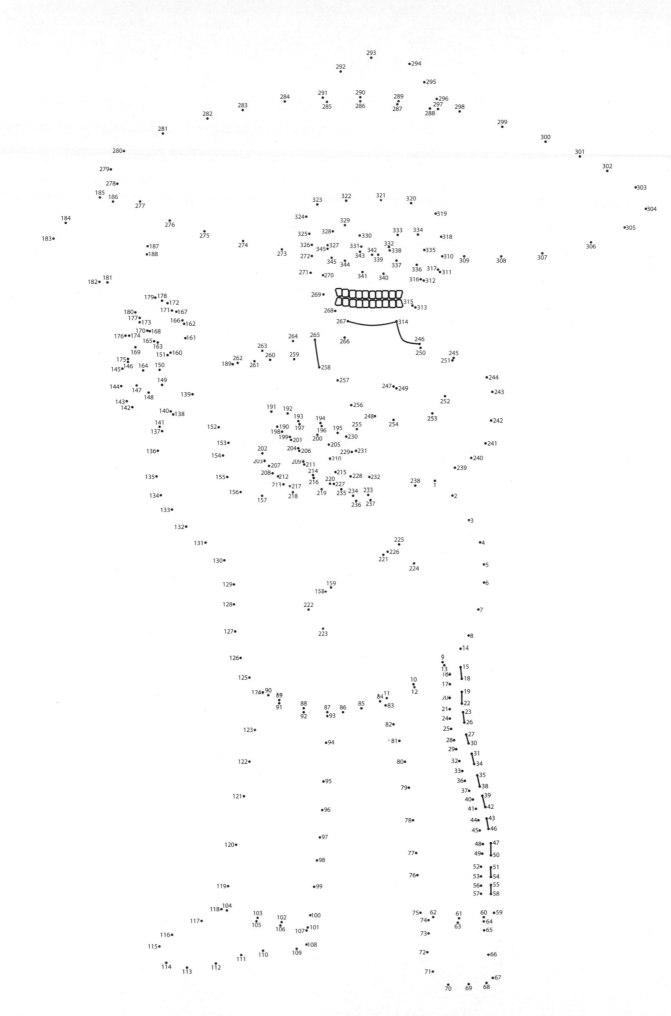

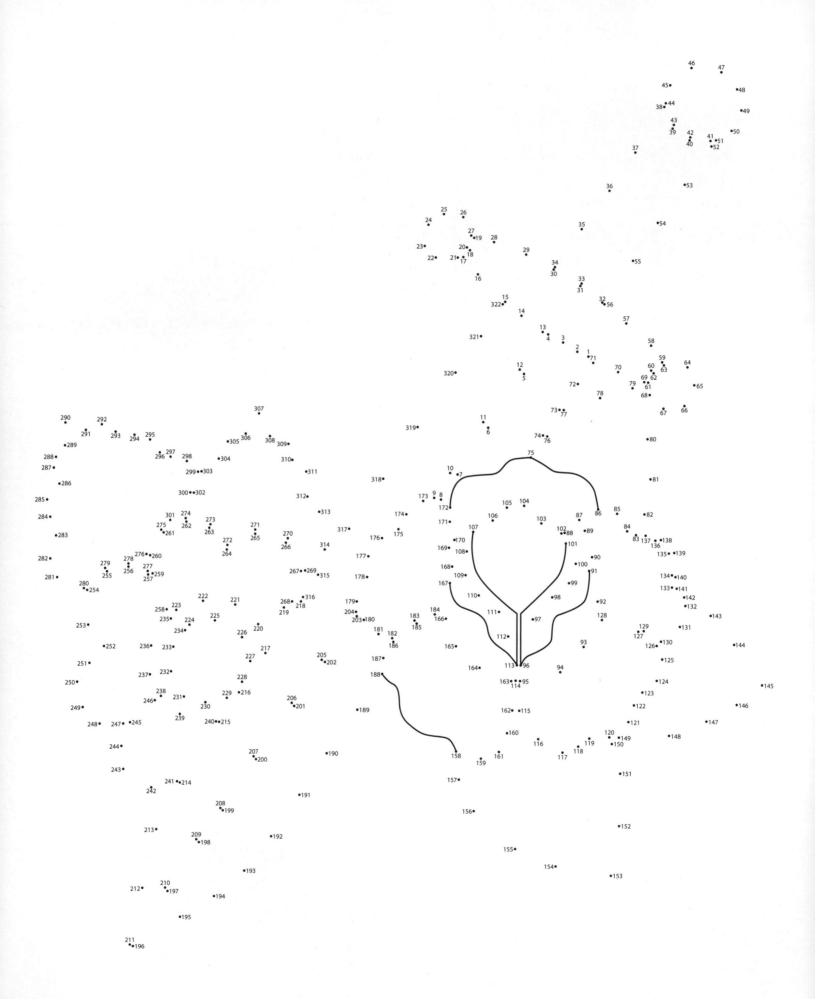

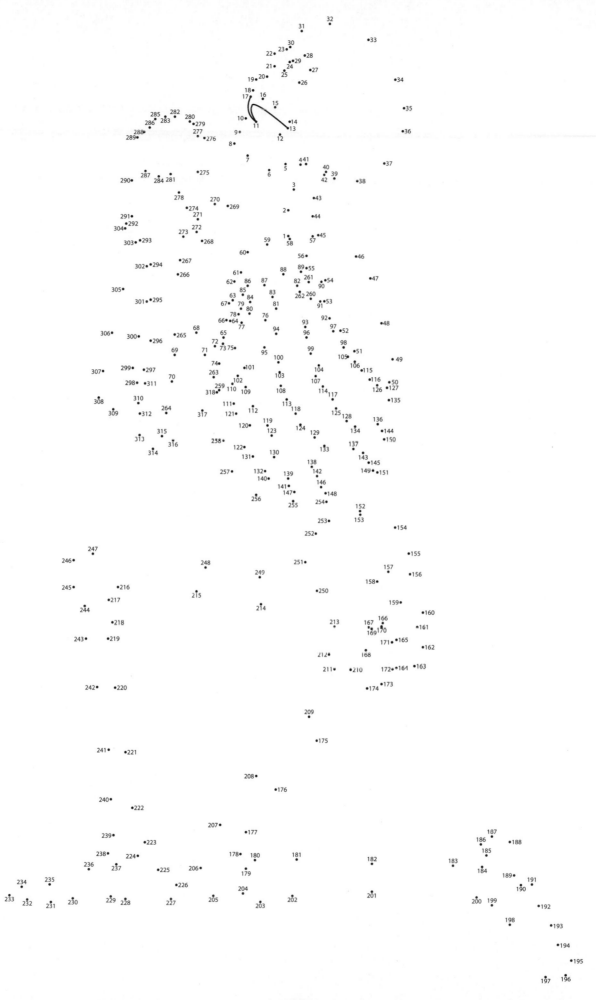

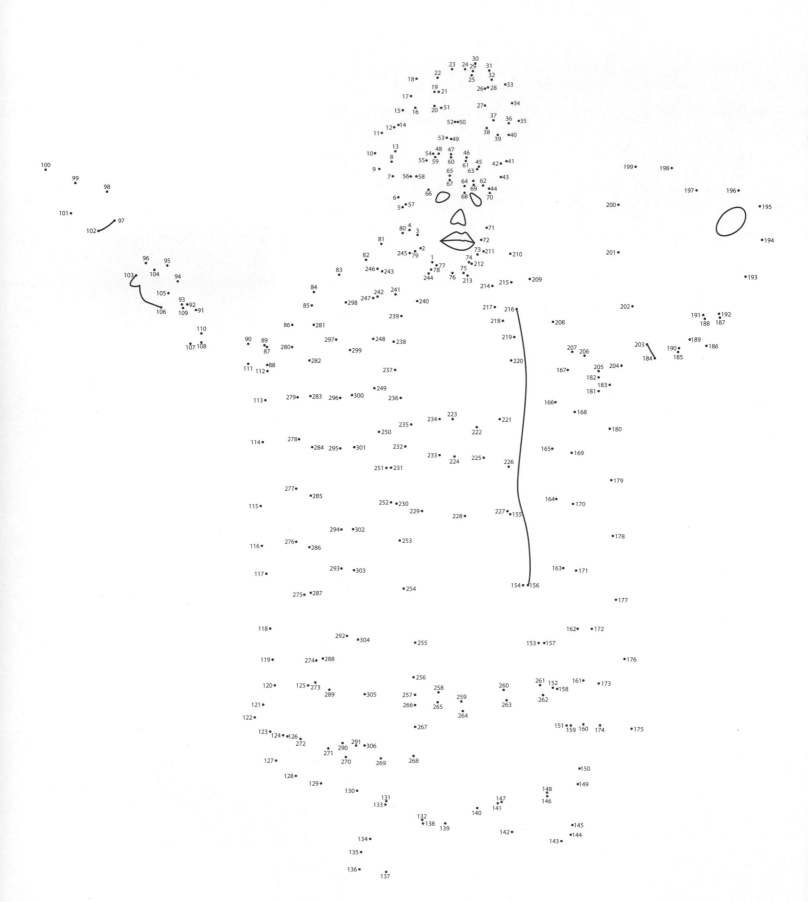

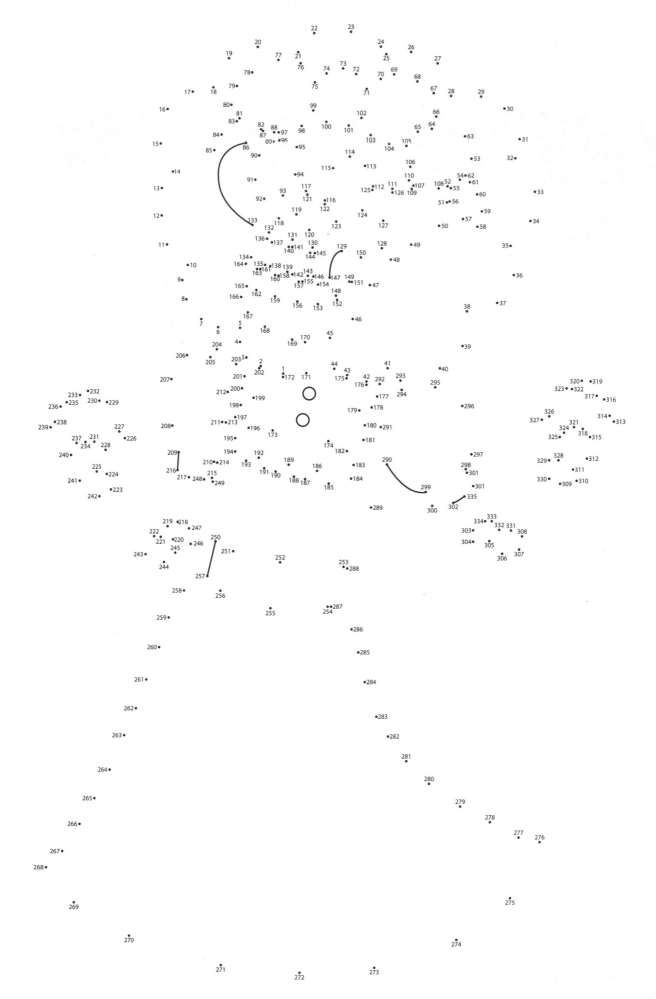

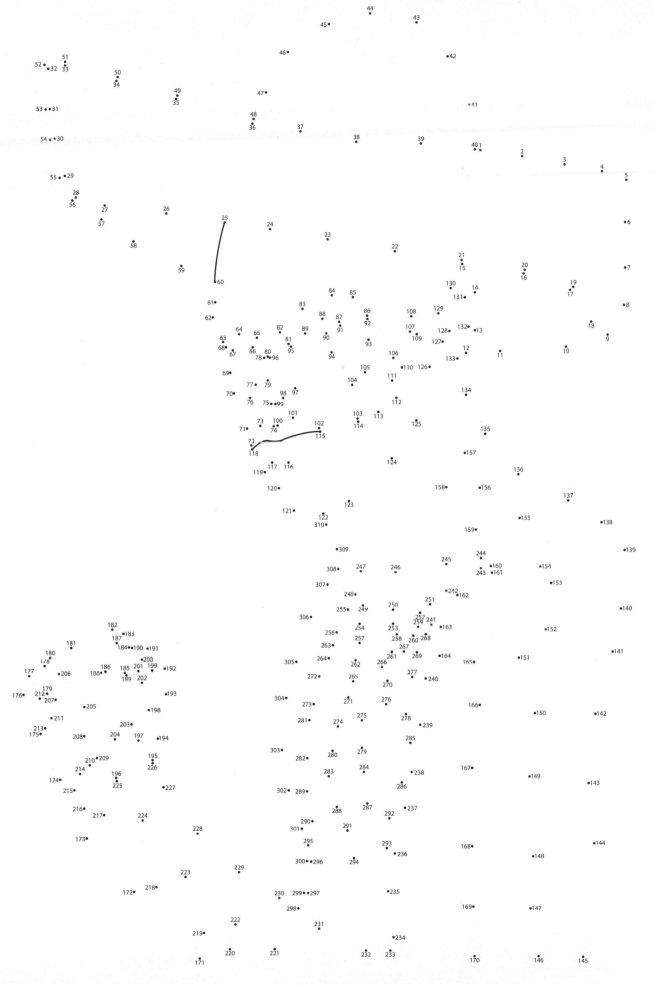

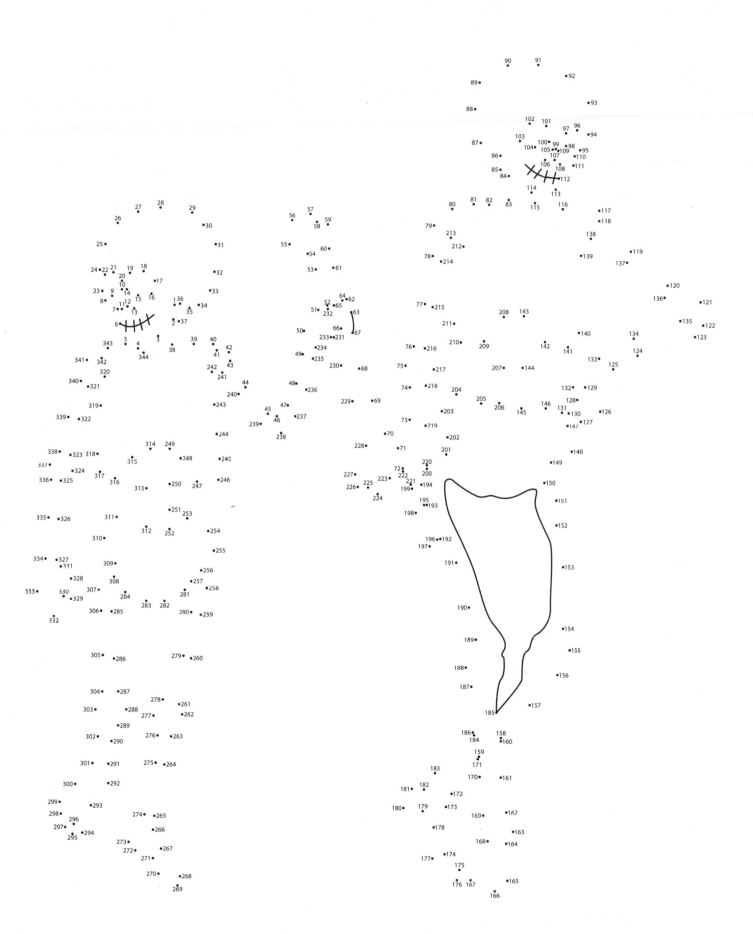

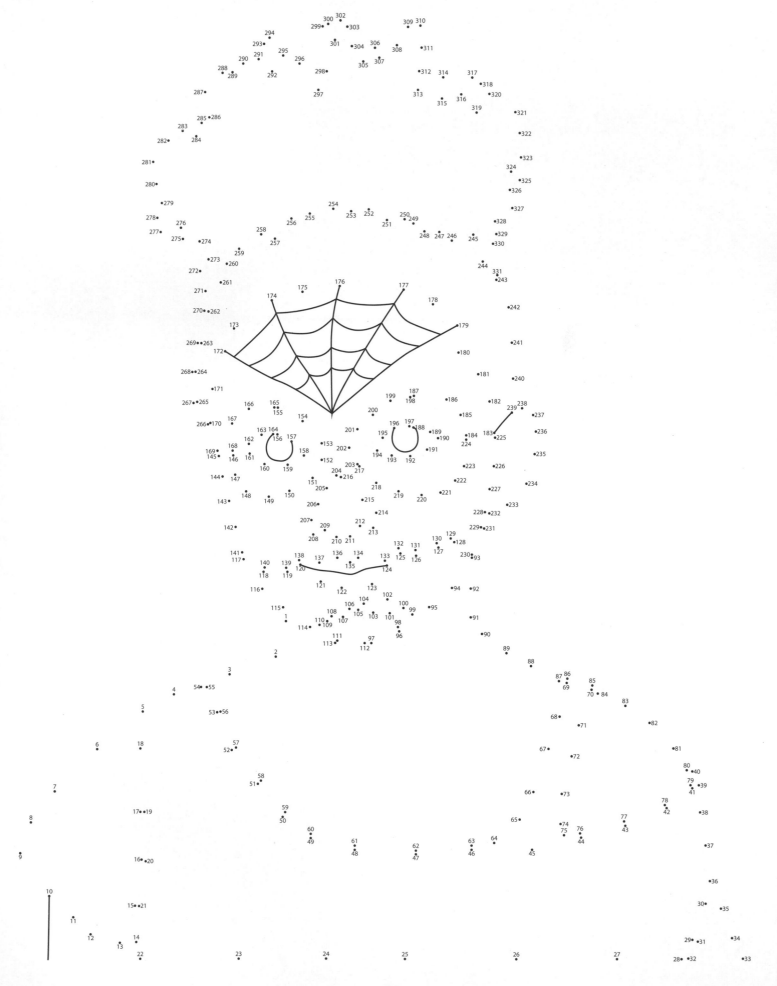

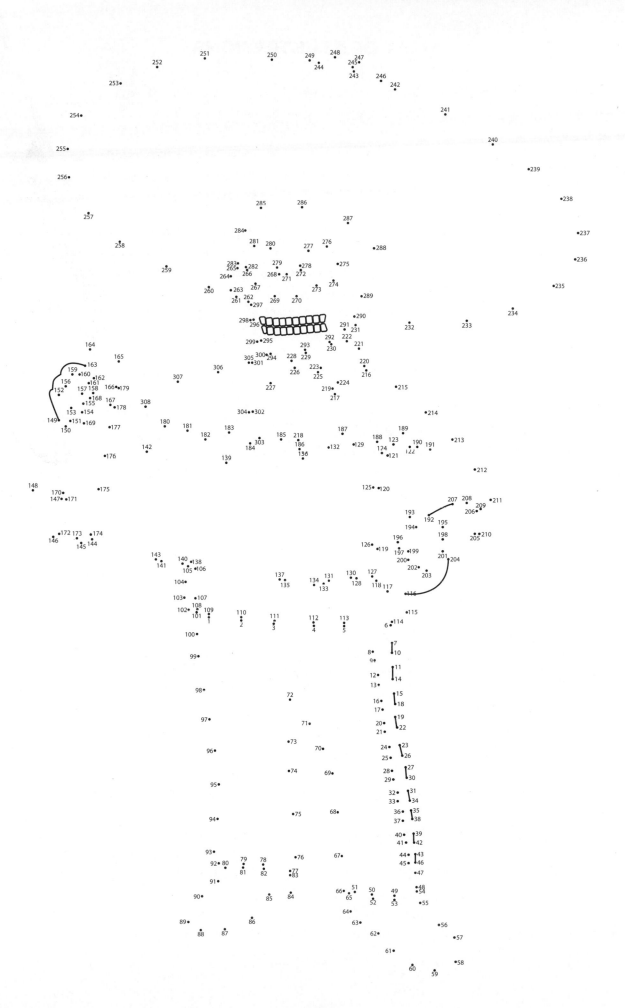

LIST OF ILLUSTRATIONS

Skeleton hand reaching for butterfly...4

Sugar skull design 1. 6

Papel picado design 1 7

Sugar skull design 2. 8

Skull with bottle and flowers. 9

Pan de Muertos 10

'Hear no evil' skeleton 11

Incense. 12

Photo frames 13

Altar 14

Sugar skull design 3. 15

Small shrine. 16

Skeleton 17

Santa Muerte (Holy Death) 18

Jesus on cross 19

A *retablo* 20

Sugar skull design 4. 21

Comparsa 22

Skeleton playing trumpet 23

Xantolo 24

Aztec/skeleton motif 1 25

Rosary 26

Mictecacihuatl 27

Papel picado design 2 28

Calacas. 29

Sugar skull design 5. 30

La Catrina. 31

Praying 32

Headstone 33

Tombs 34

Petate 35

Aztec/skeleton motif 2 36

Cemetary 37

Sugar skull design 6. 38

Angelito 39

Bird on a tombstone 40

Skeleton wearing poncho 41

Mariachi skeleton playing guitar . .42

Skeleton in tribal boots. 43

Skeleton wearing sombrero 44

Sugar skull design 7. 45

Chiapas traditional dress. 46

Danza Azteca (Aztec dance) 47

Danza Mestiza (mixed dance) 48

Jarabe Tapatio (Mexican hat dance) 49

La Danza del Venado (deer dance). .50

Sugar skull design 8. 51

Concheros 52

Skeleton marionetas 53

Mexican toys 54

Mariachi skeleton playing trumpet .55

Sugar skull design 9. 56

Skeleton arm coming out of ground .57

Aztec/skeleton motif 3 58

Woman dancing with basket
    on head 59

Cat skull 60

Skull with butterfly wings 61

Aztec skull coin 62

Mariachi skeleton playing violin. . .63

Wilted roses 64

Skull with rose in mouth. 65

Skeleton getting out of coffin 66

Sugar skull design 10 67

Skull with marigolds 68

Quijada 69

Tlapitzalli 70

Candles 71

Calaveras de Azúcar. 72

Sugar skull design 11 73

Mezcal with worm 74

Xoloitzcuintli 75

Xoloitzcuintli skeleton 76

Sugar skull design 12 77

Skeleton dolls 78

Papel picado design 3 79

Skull with floral arrangement 80

Angel with baby's breath flowers . .81

Sugar skull design 13 82

Orchids with skull 83

Aztec pyramid. 84

Cactus with cow skull 85

Desert landscape 86

Sugar skull design 14 87

Aztec/skeleton motif 4 88

Skeleton with Aztec headdress. . . .89

Sugar skull design 15 90

Skeleton holding a flower 91

Aztec skeleton. 92

Church spire 93

Woman with marigold in hair 94

Skeletons holding hands 95

Sugar skull design 16 96

Skeletons dancing. 97

Skeleton with braids & flowers . . .98

'See no evil' skeleton 99

Sugar skull design 17 100

Skeleton doing tequila shots 101

Skeleton wedding. 102

Monarch butterflies on a skull. . . 103

Skeleton riding a skeleton horse. . 104

Sugar skull design 18 105

Skull with candle on top
    dripping wax 106

Skeleton with maracas 107

Skeleton dancing with a cat 108

Girl with painted face and flowers . 109

Piñata 110

Aztec/skeleton motif 5 111

Sugar skull design 19 112

'Say no evil' skeleton 113

El atrapanovios with skeleton
    hands 114

Mariachi skeleton with guitarron . 115

Daggers with flowers 116

Skeleton praying 117

Frida skeleton 118

Sugar skull design 20 119

Skeleton girl with dress on 120

Bull skull with big horns 121

Carved pumpkin 122

Man with painted face and
    sombrero 123

Spider web pattern 124

Two skeleton children 125

Young girl with painted face 126

Mariachi skeleton with
    an accordion 127